The U.S.A. in End Times Bible Prophecy:
The Roles of Big Tech, Big Media, and Big Government

Volume 2

Earl Bristow

Copyright © 2021 Earl Bristow

All rights reserved. No part of this book may be reproduced or used in any manner without written permission of the copyright owner except for the use of quotations in a book review.

For more information:
Contact: erbrist@gmail.com

Scripture taken from the New King James Version ®.Copyright © 1982 by Thomas Nelson. Used by permission. All rights reserved.

All scriptures quoted in this publication are quoted from the New King James Bible, unless otherwise noted.

ACKNOWLEDGMENTS

I wish to thank two friends who have made this book possible.

Gerald Collins and I have been discussing the subject of this book for over a year. Without his nudging and the great material for ideas he supplied me, this book possibly would not have been written. Thank you, Gerald.

My next thank you goes to Mark Tredecim. He helped edit, organize, and expand many areas of the book. It is a much better book due to his many skills.

Mark is a new author and I encourage you to check out his book on Amazon - *The Great New Deal.* He describes it as a (not quite) fictional preview of future history. I am encouraging him to take the ideas we have been discussing and to write his next book.

Thank you Mark, for your valuable contributions.

Foreword

The liberties guaranteed under the U.S. Constitution are under direct attack from leftist ideologies, activists, and government statistics. Mandates, executive orders, and overreaching legislation from one-party rule are replacing the democratic system that served the U.S. well for nearly 250 years. Once-trusted news media and educators have lost the trust of Americans. Big finance and big business often collaborate in this assault.

Americans are asking:

- What is happening to our country?
- What can we do to save our nation and protect our families?"
- Why is God allowing all this?
- What have we done to deserve this?
- What is going to happen next?"

Many people think the Bible's End Times prophecies are too hard to understand, so they don't try. A three-headed beast of Big Tech, Big Media, and Big Government threatens the American republic and its people.

Fortunately, the book also provides good news. It describes how all of this fits perfectly within God's plan for the End Times and how this is leading to the outcome promised in the Bible: God wins, evil loses.

Table of Contents

THE U.S.A. IN END TIMES BIBLE PROPHECY: I
COPYRIGHT © 2021 EARL BRISTOW II
ACKNOWLEDGMENTS III
FOREWORD IV
TABLE OF CONTENTS V
CHAPTER 1   INTRODUCTION 1
CHAPTER 2   *IN THE BEGINNING* OF THE BIBLE 16
CHAPTER 3   *IN THE BEGINNING* OF THE UNITED STATES OF AMERICA 19
CHAPTER 4   WHAT DOES THE BIBLE SAY ABOUT CAPITALISM, SOCIALISM, AND GOVERNMENT? 25
CHAPTER 5   BIG TECH: THE BEGINNING 39
CHAPTER 6   BIG TECH: THE FUTURE 55
CHAPTER 7   BIG MEDIA 73
CHAPTER 8   BIG GOVERNMENT 89
CHAPTER 9   HOW SOCIALISM WILL INCREASE IN AMERICA 100
CHAPTER 10 BIBLE PROPHECY 120
CHAPTER 11 CLOSING COMMENTS 131
CONCLUDING THOUGHTS 137
A THANK YOU FROM THE AUTHOR 139
GLOSSARY OF TERMS 140
BOOKS BY EARL BRISTOW 146
ENDNOTES / BIBLIOGRAPHY 148

Chapter 1

Introduction

Fact or Fiction?

Many people do not believe the end of the age Jesus and the prophets described in Bible prophecy. They discredit the description of the prophesied one-world government that will be ruled by one man – the Antichrist. They do not believe a loving God will destroy billions of people and to buy and sell they must take the *mark of the beast or they will be beheaded (Revelation 20:24)*. These descriptions of the end of age frighten people.

Many people call these events fictional tales because it will be impossible to establish a one worldwide government to control buying and selling.

If you believe the Bible, these events are destined to happen here in the United States.

Current evolving events are making the United States unknowingly a key player to make some of these events feasible – especially controlling buying and selling. It may seem like fiction or a bad dream, but if you examine how the Chinese government is using technology to control over a billion people, it is possible.

Will it occur here in the U.S?

This book will enlighten you on how it could happen.

Big Tech, Big Media, and Big Government are powerful forces in the U.S.A. Together, they evoke the image of the hydra, a horrifying multi-headed beast in Greek mythology.

The hydra in Greek mythology was a many-headed serpent or monster that was ultimately slain by Hercules. The hydra instilled fear in its adversaries because each head possessed unique powers of destruction. Whenever one head was cut off, two others replaced it.

The Roles of Big Tech, Big Media, and Big Government

An analogy to the *Perfect Storm* movie is used to metaphorically depict a three-headed hydra of Big Tech, Big Media, and Big Government converging as a powerful Perfect Political Storm preceding the end of the age.

A thirty-year veteran meteorologist, Bob Case, of the National Oceanic and Atmospheric Administration (NOAA) Boston office described to author Sebastian Junger a large high-pressure system over Canada, a low-pressure system traveling along a slow-moving cold front, and Hurricane Grace converging simultaneously. Junger coined the conditions as *"The Perfect Storm"* for his 1997 book about the 1991 storm and the crew of the boat Andrea Gail.[1]

In 2000, *The Perfect Storm* movie was released (starring George Clooney and Mark Wahlberg), loosely based upon the book. The movie producers claimed it was based on a true story, and the movie's web site declared that the storm was "a unique event in recorded history where three storms were combined into one, heaping waves 100-feet high, creating nothing less than an almost apocalyptic situation."

Captain Billy Tyne in the movie *The Perfect Storm* tried valiantly to navigate the Andrea Gale, his seventy-seven-foot-long commercial fishing boat, through the raging seas of a nor-easter to return home to Gloucester, Massachusetts from an extremely successful fishing expedition.

Captain Tyne and his crew were caught in the horns of a dilemma - their ice machine had failed, and if they retreated to safer waters, their highly perishable and valuable cargo of fresh swordfish would spoil. Each man would share in the large financial rewards from their great haul of fish, so the crew agreed to forge ahead into the heart of a ferocious storm.

After they sailed into the storm, they realized it was hopeless to believe the ship could withstand 40-foot waves with winds howling at more than 50 mph. Each crew member knew the Andrea Gail would sink if they continued this course. They miraculously turned the ship around to sail in the opposite direction so it could run with the storm. Unknown to them, their new course took them into the eye of Hurricane Grace.

The calm seas in the eye made them feel they were safe. According to the movie, suddenly the crew of the Andrea Gail stared in horror at a 100-foot wave cresting in front of them - they were sailing into a category 5 hurricane with sustained wind speeds of more than 150 miles per hour and 100-foot waves. The gigantic waves flipped the Andrea Gail from fore to aft. To this day, the ship and its crew have never been recovered.[2]

According to factual weather accounts, Hurricane Grace was at best a category 2 hurricane. The "100-foot" waves were probably in the 25 to 50 range.[3] Even without these dramatic exaggerations in the movie, the actual weather conditions spelled doom for the crew of the Andrea Gail.

The movie's exaggerations made for great movie effects, and the film was nominated for two Academy Awards: Best Sound and Best Visual Effects. The great majority of the people who watched the movie never suspected it was overhyped. The Perfect Storm was a box office success despite mixed reviews from critics.

After the film was released, the families of two crew members sued the film makers for the fictionalization of events prior to the loss of Andrea Gail. Some unnamed families also sued because the facts were changed. A district court in Florida dismissed the case because the judge ruled the movie writers' First Amendment right to freedom of speech barred the suit. The families eventually lost their appeals.[4]

This story of the disaster facing the crew of the Andrea Gail and the hyperbole used by the movie makers to promote a film with less-than-truthful facts resemble the situation the citizens of the United States are facing today.

We the people" of the United States are in a monumental battle with a modern-day hydra trying to gain control over our lifestyles.

Big Tech and Big Media disseminate misinformation, (also known as "fake news") daily to promote their own agendas, influence politicians, or add profits to their financial statements. So much fake news is being disseminated that the truth is being obscured.

The modern three-headed hydra threatening the United States is like the nor-easter the Andrea Gail sailed into. The events occurring in our nation have been slowly developing for years, but now they are like a hurricane unleashing a mighty force of destruction. Our nation is being hit with the *"Perfect Political Storm."*

The era of instant internet access through Facebook (now META), Twitter (now X), WhatsApp, Instagram, TikTok, and cable news provides people with so much information and misinformation so fast, that determining fact from fiction is practically impossible.

The most graphic modern-day example of media controlling our emotions started in 2020 with the outbreak of COVID-19. First, it was COVID-19 and then its mutations – Delta and Omicron. Unprecedented amounts of contradictory information were disseminated over every type of media channel by politicians, doctors, and citizens. Some challenged the effectiveness of masks, others question whether there were risks in taking a vaccine that was rushed through for approval by the Federal Drug Administration. Others questioned the seemingly low priority given to research and use of non-vaccine solutions (preventative and therapeutic) and propose using alternative drugs like ivermectin.

The Centers for Disease Control (CDC) has damaged its credibility by issuing contradictory, inconsistent, and confusing advisories. Information indicates that CDC leaders knew about risky coronavirus research in Wuhan facilities, financed some of it and covered up the origins of COVID-19 and their involvement. Serious questions arise in people's minds due to this. This does not build trust in the CDC or its leaders. In addition, FBI Director Christopher Wray stated before Congress in March 2023, "COVID-19 was most likely a lab incident in China."[5]

Big Government and Big Media repeatedly broadcast during the pandemic an even more deadly variant than Delta and Omicron could mutate. An article in Newsweek on August 4, 2021 describes a potential variant as *"Doomsday."* Here is an excerpt from that article:

"...will the Lambda (variant) turn out to be the next big, bad thing that COVID-19 unleashes on us? It is a good time to wonder: Just how destructive can these variants get? Will future variants expand their attack from the lungs to the brain, the heart, and other organs? Will they take a page from HIV and trick people into thinking they have recovered, only to make them sick later? Is there a *Doomsday* variant out there that shrugs off vaccines, spreads like wildfire and leaves more of its victims much sicker than anything we have yet seen?"[6]

Was the Newsweek article fear-mongering to sell magazines? Or was the article supported by scientific evidence that is truthful and accurate? If it was factual, why were the sources not cited? Overwhelming, the news media predicted science indicated a more powerful strand could mutate.

In September 2021, President Biden set forth more requirements with the premise that unvaccinated people need to be vaccinated to protect vaccinated people. The government's battle plan for COVID-19 relied heavily on *vaccine mandates, vaccine passports, mask mandates, mandatory testing, and other requirements*. Enforcement of these new conditions laid the foundation for future government control by taking away our freedoms granted in the U.S. Constitution.

Consider the following comparison of two pandemics.

As September 2023, the global COVID-19 death count has exceeded 6.9 million. This is a tragedy because each person matters to God.

Now compare that to the "Black Death" pandemic. In the 1300's, there was a multi-year bubonic plague pandemic that struck Africa, Asia, and Europe. If contracted, the mortality rate was estimated at about 80%. It struck some nations more intensely, but the percentage of the population killed was generally in double digits, ranging from 10% to 50%. This first wave was followed by major periodic bubonic plague outbreaks for another 400+ years. Estimates of the number of deaths range from 75 to 200 million people died during those years.

COVID-19 has been a major disaster, but on God's End Times scale, should this be considered a category 1 or 2 pandemic? If it is only a 1 or 2, can you imagine what devastation a category 5 will cause?

Prophecies in the Bible book of Revelation describe an upcoming seven-year period called the Tribulation when God will unleash His holy judgments on this sinful world. Estimates of the number of people to die by violence, famine, plague, and at the battle of Armageddon range from 60% to 70% of the total world population (Revelation 6, 9, and 19) – possibly as many as 6 billion people.

The liberal elements of Big Media wanted to control us by embedding fear of contracting COVID-19 into our minds on their daily broadcasts so they could increase their audience size and network ratings. Simultaneously, we had to contend with fears from rising crime, riots, and police brutality. To cope with these fears, millions of Americans started looking to Congress and the President to ease their fears by marshaling the power of the U.S. government to alter their circumstances and ensure their safety.

In addition, multiple organizations are promoting ideologies that seek to destroy our most sacred individual rights to freedom of worship, freedom of speech, and freedom from political persecution that are contained in the Bill of Rights. Sadly, a New York Times funded project, *The 1619 Project*, was released on November 15, 2021. Its aim is to rewrite U.S. history and demonize many of our national heroes. It uses the issue of slavery as a lever to disrupt race relations in the United States.

People in the United States are in a similar situation to Captain Tyne in the Perfect Storm movie. With all the information and misinformation (fake news) bombarding us, how do we discern what is truthful and accurate? Which course will we take to avoid the storm?

In the *Perfect Storm* movie, the Andrea Gail turned away from the nor-easter and sailed into the calm of the eye of Hurricane Grace. The crew thought they were going to be safe. Millions of people are presently expressing their desire for our government to embrace socialism and provide all their needs for health care along with a minimum guaranteed income. They are unknowingly becoming like the crew of the Andrea Gale when they entered the eye of the hurricane – disaster would soon strike.

Have you ever read the book *1984* (published in 1949)? If you have not, it is an excellent time to read (or reread) it. The author George Orwell (who ironically favored the theory of "democratic socialism" but had observed the real-life socialist tyrannies of Nazi Germany and the Soviet bloc) introduces a future totalitarian government in the year 1984, which displayed posters everywhere stating *"Big Brother Is Watching You."* These posters were a constant reminder that the government exercised total control over the people in the fictional land of Oceania. The government watched every citizen in their homes, at work, walking on the streets, and travelling in commercial vehicles through a sophisticated network of cameras and telescreens.

The focal character of the book is Winston Smith who becomes disenchanted with the government controlling his life. His job in the Ministry of Truth was to change the record of past historical events and rewrite them so they aligned to the government's current dogma. He was just one of a host of writers working to change peoples' perception of the past. By this means, the government altered the past to align it with their present plans and propaganda.

Smith's job was closely aligned with the regime's Newspeak - Big Brother's official language through which the government would control what people say and think without them realizing it. Thousands of people were engaged by the Oceania government to eliminate, redefine, and simplify the words people used to better control their minds and thoughts. The goal was to eliminate and change the meanings of the words so that people would not be able to use words to have "bad thoughts."

The book *1984* describes the implementation of technologies like distributed cameras and remote monitoring sites that are being installed today in the United States and other countries around the world. Governments are installing security cameras on streets and government facilities. Cameras and security check-points are being added within commercial buildings across the nation. Automated traffic cameras, license plate readers, and toll road cameras are being used in many jurisdictions.

Many people are installing home video security systems, like Ring, with cameras that record to the internet cloud and can transmit video images to the homeowner's cell phone. Smart TV's have cameras which can be remotely turned on to enable transmission of images over the internet. Cell phones with cameras, GPS-tracking, and recording capability are carried by nearly everyone in the U.S. and in most nations around the world. Facial recognition technology is advancing and is already being used in some nations to monitor people.

Google Assistant, Siri from Apple, and Alexa from Amazon enable you with a simple voice command, to set alarms, reminders, play music, answer questions, search the internet, and control smart home devices. They can also tell you jokes, provide interesting facts, and even play games with you. However, they also can spy on you. Here is a summary of a lawsuit filed against Apple, Google, and Amazon that is proceeding in federal courts as this book was published.

Apple, Google, Amazon spying on you, lawsuits claim

> **Big Tech is listening to your private discussions, lawsuits claim. Should you be worried?**
>
> A federal judge has given a green light for a class-action lawsuit claiming that Apple's Siri voice assistant violates users' privacy.
>
> In August 2021, U.S. District Judge Jeffrey White said the plaintiffs would be allowed to move forward with lawsuits trying to prove that Siri routinely recorded their private conversations because of "accidental activations" and that Apple provided the conversations to advertisers, according to Reuters. The plaintiffs claim that Apple violated the Federal Wiretap Act and California privacy law, among other claims.
>
> Separate lawsuits against Google and Amazon make similar claims about voice assistants. One of the most common claims cited in the lawsuits is that conversations were recorded without user consent and then used by advertisers to target the plaintiffs.

In 2022, there were around 142 million users of voice assistants in the United States, nearly half of the country's population. The number of voice assistant users is forecast to increase to 157.1 million users in 2026.[7]

ChatGPT is being used to generate human-resembling text responses from text prompts to generate responses from its wide dataset. Google Bard AI and Microsoft Bing Chat offer similar capabilities.

The diverse range of functionalities and applications of includes:

- Answering questions
- Language translation
- Writing assistance
- Creative writing
- Learning and education
- Personal assistance
- Entertainment

Smart refrigerators already have installed computer chips. The expectation is the next generation of refrigerators will have a camera to scan the barcodes codes of the products in it to provide a continual inventory to your online grocery store.

Driverless cars with RFID tags connect to the internet so you can be charged for toll roads.

The hydra knows who you are, what you are doing, and who you talk to. They know what you listen to and read. They know how far you walk every day, your heart rate, and glucose levels.

Big Brother will know every aspect of your life.

Unless you live completely "off the grid" in some remote place where you are completely self-sustaining (and don't need medical care), your privacy will be gone. Probably, Big Tech has more of your privacy information than you think!

All of your digital information is being stored and scrutinized. It is being shared and used (legally or otherwise) by *Big Tech, Big Government, and Big Business.* Your data is commonly referred to as "big data." To make things worse, foreign governments and cybercriminals often gain access to this information and they are using it for their own evil purposes.

If this doesn't get your attention, let me turn your attention to what the Federal Government has done over the last few years.

In January 2023, the ongoing publication of the Twitter Files, a serial investigation into the way the company has managed sensitive public issues, commissioned by its new owner, Elon Musk. Not long after Musk bought Twitter, in October, he reached out to a few prominent journalists, each of them at least broadly sympathetic to Musk's view that Twitter's past moderation decisions reflected its own entrenchment in the liberal establishment, and were therefore effectively suppressing conservative and other dissenting views.

Musk opened internal Twitter memos to Taibbi, Bari Weiss, Michael Shellenberger, and reporter Lee Fang. Their revelations became known as the Twitter Files were chilling and eye opening to the degree the Federal Government was attempting to control the flow of information. It will be discussed in the Big Government chapter.

As more Congressional Oversight hearings have been held in 2022 and 2023, more disturbing information has been revealed. In July 2023, Federal Judge Terry Doughty issued a preliminary injunction that restricts the Biden administration from manipulating and pressuring social media outlets for its own messaging purposes. This important ruling will be covered in the Big Government chapter.

Our nation is closer to the *"Beware Big Brother Is Watching You"* reality than you think. Some countries like China and North Korea are implementing programs today that enable them to control their citizens actions ranging from where they travel, what they buy, what web sites they view, and the list goes on and on.

Scary? You bet!

We are living in a time like thousands of years ago described in the Bible when humanity set out to build a magnificent tower – the Tower of Babel - reaching into the heavens.

> "⁴Come, let us build ourselves a city, and a tower whose top is in the heavens; let us make a name for ourselves, lest we be scattered abroad over the face of the whole earth." (Genesis 11:4)

Today Big Tech, medical doctors, and scientists have become the architects of a modern-day Tower of Babel. The sharing of advancements in technology are making it possible to achieve new breakthroughs in an ever-shortening time-span. The exponential growth of advanced technology is giving humans unprecedented control over the physical world. God knew this would occur and even had the prophet Daniel proclaim over 2,500 years ago this would happen (Daniel 12:4).

God made a statement about the people building the tower that applies today:

> "⁶...what they begin to do; now nothing that they propose to do will be withheld from them." (Genesis 11:6)

God permitted the people to build the tower for a time, but gave the people different languages and then he scattered the people to distant lands which effectively stopped the building (Genesis 11:9). Today, God is permitting humanity to continue unabated with their incredible advancements for a season, but only until His plan is complete. The end is very, very near.

Satan also has a plan for his war against God. Satan loves using humanity as his pawns and to use human-developed advanced technology against God. The age-old battle between good and evil will continue until the End of Times. Control of humanity is at the center of this battle.

Big Government's, Big Tech's, and Big Media's convergence into a *Perfect Political Storm* will pale in comparison to a real category 5 plus hurricane that is coming – *God's Ultimate Perfect Storm*. This storm is going to slam into the United States and the world as prophesied in the Bible at the predicted End Times.

Bible skeptics are unaware God's plan to redeem humanity is quickly approaching fulfillment. God will use the combined efforts of Big Tech,

The Roles of Big Tech, Big Media, and Big Government

Big Media, and Big Government to help establish the one world government which He will eventually destroy.

Volume one of this series, *The U.S.A. in Bible Prophecy,* explores the role the United States will play in End Times. It may surprise you that the U.S. will not be a major world power. Please consider reading it – I think you will find it interesting. It is on Amazon.

The supreme God of Heaven and Earth described in the Bible has a plan to redeem humanity and establish His perfect kingdom on Earth. Non-believers in God scoff at the idea that a loving and caring God sent his Son Jesus to die for their sins, that He has a plan for their lives, and that He desires a personal relationship with them.

There are other people who are sincere believers in God and have a personal relationship with Him; but have difficulty understanding End Times events (described primarily in the books of Daniel and Revelation). These people do not yet recognize or accept the truth that cataclysmic events described in the Bible will occur, and bring an end to our current era (my prayer is that after a careful reading of my books and the referenced Bible passages, many will open their hearts and minds to believe in Jesus and that He is coming soon). Here are the major events many people do not understand or find them unbelievable:

- the Rapture of the Christian church
- the seven years of Tribulation
- the Battle of Armageddon
- Jesus Christ returns to set up His Millennial Kingdom on earth.

Equally hard or impossible for many people to believe is the Biblically described rise of one man – the Antichrist – who will be given power from all national governments to rule the world during the seven years of Tribulation. They also cannot believe a world government will be able to control all buying and selling.

To counter the argument that these events are not going to happen, let's remember how the Bible described historical events hundreds (even thousands) of years before they happened. Here is a sampling of major prophecies that were fulfilled precisely and are backed up with facts that can be verified by historical references other than the Bible:

- Old Testament prophets declared the nation of Israel would be judged for their sins, Israel would be defeated by foreign armies, and the people would be exiled to foreign lands. This occurred when the Assyrians defeated Israel in approximately 732 B.C. Then the Babylonians defeated Judea in approximately 597 B.C. and destroyed the Temple in 586 B.C.

- Jeremiah prophesied that Judah's captivity in Babylon would last 70 years. The Jews returned to Jerusalem in the first year of Cyrus of Persia exactly seventy years later.

- Daniel prophesied in about 539 B. C. a future decree would be issued to restore and rebuild Jerusalem and the Temple. The Temple was completed in 515 B.C. He also prophesied that a period of 173,880 days would elapse until the date when the Anointed One (the Messiah) would come. Years later, King Artaxerxes of Persia gave that order in 445 B.C. and 173,880 days later, Jesus rode into Jerusalem on the back of a donkey colt (fulfilling yet another prophecy) and was proclaimed by the people to be the Messiah, a day we celebrate as "Palm Sunday."

- Jesus declared in approximately 30 A.D. the Temple in Jerusalem would be destroyed and Israel would no longer exist as a nation. This happened about forty years later when Rome destroyed the Temple and Israel was totally defeated in 70 A.D.

- The prophet Isiah prophesied nearly 2,700 years ago that the nation of Israel would be restored in a single day. This happened on May 14, 1948, when the United Nations declared Israel would become a nation once again after nearly 2,000 years. Today, Jerusalem is their capital, Hebrew is the official language, Jews have the right to immigrate there, and they celebrate Shabbat and their Jewish holidays.

The Roles of Big Tech, Big Media, and Big Government

If you grow in your understanding of what the Bible says, you will be able to better understand the social and geo-political climate we live in today – you will have a new understanding of the events unfolding before your eyes. The Bible is not a fiction book and accurately describes future events!

Humanity's enemy, Satan, wants you to ignore the Bible and declare Bible prophecy to be a myth. Satan's primary weapon has always been lies and deception, which started in the garden of Eden with Adam and Eve. Big Tech, Big Media, and Big Government have increased the means Satan has available to deceive modern humanity. Each time Jesus talked about the End Times, he ended the discourse with a warning - "*do not be deceived.*"

> "*[8]He replied: <u>Watch out that you are not deceived</u>. For many will come in my name, claiming, I am he, and, The time is near." Do not follow them.*" (Luke 21:8)

We are living in a time where the truth has become subjective, so what was once considered the truth is now being relabeled as a lie. The Bible described the time we are living in this way:

> "*[20]Woe to those who call evil good, and good evil.*" (Isaiah 5:20)

Satan's power is limited. Satan did not know that God would raise Jesus from the dead as part of His plan to have his Son die for the sins of humanity. Nor did Satan know that all who believed in Jesus would receive eternal life.

Alone, Satan cannot develop the tools needed to implement his new world order, control a one-world government, and establish the one-world religion he desires. So, he enlists mankind to do it. Satan likely enjoys the idea of turning man (created in God's image) against his Creator. The Bible in Revelation 13 describes a multi-headed beast (reminiscent of the hydra monster) that will use men and human institutions to make war against God's people and exercise dominion over them.

One of the definitions of the heart that is commonly used refers to a person's character, or the place within a person where feelings or emotions come from, e.g., he broke her heart; I love you with all my heart; he died of a broken heart. The Bible clearly uses this definition of heart to describe the source of deceit, wickedness, and evil plans.

> *"¹⁷The heart is deceitful above all things, And desperately wicked; Who can know it?" (Jeremiah 17:9)*

> *"¹⁴Perversity is in his heart, He devises evil continually, He sows discord." (Proverbs 6:14)*

This book focuses on how a hydra with a heart full of deceit will empower the heads of Big Tech, Big Media, and Big Government to converge and _unknowingly_ provide Satan with the technology and tools to implement his plan to rule through a new world order controlled by the Antichrist.

A brief review of God's plan for humanity and Satan's plan to disrupt it will be provided in the next chapter.

As you read and hear about events happening today, you are probably asking yourself:

> "Is there any hope for America?"

> "Is there hope for me?"

Just like his unsuccessful attempts to kill Jesus, first using Herod's soldiers in Bethlehem and later using Roman soldiers for the crucifixion, Satan's plan to rule the world will fail. The Bible tells us how - in the end God wins and Satan loses. If you possess the knowledge that God is going to win, this should give you HOPE for a brighter day and tomorrow. Here is a great quote:

> "For the believer there is hope beyond the grave, because Jesus Christ has opened the door to heaven for us by His death and resurrection." - Billy Graham

Chapter 2

"In the Beginning" of the Bible

"In the beginning" are the first three words in Genesis Chapter 1 of the Bible.

The book of Genesis explains how God created the heavens and earth. Then God created light, darkness, the seas, dry land, grass, trees, day, night, living creatures in the sea, and on land. God desired companionship and created Adam and Eve in His image to fellowship with Him. They lived in the Garden of Eden and God supplied their every need in this paradise. They were to tend and keep the Garden, and they had only one command to obey:

> *"[17]of the tree of the knowledge of good and evil you shall not eat, for in the day that you eat of it you shall surely die." (Genesis 1:17)*

God's desire was for Adam and Eve to live in contentment tending the Garden. Satan was one of God's highest-ranking angels prior to the sin of Adam and Eve, but was expelled by God from heaven because He desired to be like God.

God also knew that Satan would tempt Adam and Eve, and they would disobey His simple command. When Eve took the bite out of the forbidden fruit, the battle for the souls of all humanity began. However, God knew in advance this would happen, and He began unveiling His plan to establish His kingdom, where people who choose to believe in Him will live in paradise for eternity without any temptations from Satan.

God's prophecies depict the End Times events necessary for Satan to carry out his plan to rule the world. For the nations and people to hand over to Satan and the Antichrist the ability to control the world, death and destruction must be so devastating the people will do anything to live in peace. The Tribulation events will be so intense that nations and people will do anything to seek peace and avoid destruction. Many people will turn to Jesus Christ as savior. But most people and all of the nations will be persuaded that the only safe path to peace comes through Satan's minion, the Antichrist, and his worldwide rule.

If you have not read any of my books about the End Times, I encourage you to do so. The *End of the World* series can be found on Amazon and the five books describe Bible prophecy in detail. They are written to be easily understood, yet deep mysteries of the Bible are unraveled. They are on Amazon.

The following summary is a consolidated view of events preceding Satan's final attempts to take over the world.

When does the Final End Times countdown begin?

Great question!

The End Times countdown began on May 14, 1948, when the United Nations voted to create the nation of Israel. Israel had not existed as a nation for nearly 1900 years.

Psalm 102 states that as Zion (Jerusalem) is being rebuilt, the Lord will appear in His glory. It then says, *"this shall be written for the generation to come."* The Hebrew word for *to come* can be translated *as the last generation* or *the terminal generation*.

If you are unfamiliar with terminologies like End Times, Rapture, or Tribulation; they and other biblical terms are explained in the Glossary. My use of these terms may differ from what you have been taught, so I encourage you to spend a few minutes becoming familiar with these terms.

Satan does not possess God's power – Satan cannot create a human being. Though he wants to be God, he is not God. Satan needs to use men and women to execute his plan for a new world order consisting of a one-world government and one-world religion.

After the Rapture when hundreds of millions of people instantly vanish from the earth, the world falls into chaos, looting, killing, and total turmoil. Shortly after the Rapture, the Antichrist assumes a position of power in a confederation of nations, possibly the European Union

The Roles of Big Tech, Big Media, and Big Government

(EU), or the United Nations. The Antichrist offers "peace," but only if the nations of the world agree to form a one-world government.

This government will initially enable order to be established. The Antichrist will take control of the best computer systems (or nationalize them) and adapt them to support the controls he wants implemented. Therefore, these systems must be up and running immediately so there is no development required and minimal time to implement minor changes.

The citizens of the United States can become unruly and confrontational when threatened with tyrannical rule like they did in the Revolutionary War and when Japan bombed Pearl Harbor in 1941. Satan does not want to have to deal with a strong-willed nation like the U.S., one that might not want to join his one-world government. Therefore, he is promoting a plan to change the America we love by causing us to become comfortable with the government issuing mandates for our safety and betterment so we will follow them like lost sheep.

Big Tech, Big Media, and Big Government are touting plans to make our lives better with the federal government paving the way by embracing a change to more socialism. They are extolling the need and benefits of Medicare for all, increased benefits for the elderly, massive aid to families, and guaranteed annual incomes. The new benefits are being proposed without any serious dialogue about how they will increase inflation, their long-term impact on the national debt, and how they impact the ability of the government treasury to pay out entitlement benefits like Social Security and Medicare.

In the next chapter, the reasons that our founding fathers put controls and balances into place will be explained, and why the present agenda being proposed is not what they envisioned.

> "Within the covers of the Bible are the answers for all the problems men face." Ronald Reagan.

Chapter 3

"In the Beginning" of the United States of America

"In the beginning" the first colony of settlers came from Great Britain in 1607 and landed in what is now Jamestown, Virginia to escape religious persecution and have political freedom. Great Britain quickly realized there were great opportunities to increase their wealth and power in North America if they established colonies along the Atlantic coast, and declared them to be part of the British empire. Thousands of settlers came seeking land and opportunity as well as to have religious freedom.

The group of Christians we call the Pilgrims meant to colonize New York, but got off-course and landed in what is now called Massachusetts. They established some key tenets for the future United States, including popular self-government and religious freedom, through the Mayflower Compact, signed aboard the good ship Mayflower in November 1620.

The colonies flourished, but the British government imposed increasingly harsh taxes on the settlers. They forced colonists to obey the laws of England as subjects of King George III instead of permitting the colonists to follow the local charters and laws they tried to establish.

Anger and resentment toward the British for imposing "taxation without representation" culminated in the Boston Tea Party. It was a political protest that occurred on December 16, 1773, in the harbor of Boston, Massachusetts. Samuel Adams organized frustrated and angry American colonists and they dumped 342 chests of the British East India Company's tea into the harbor.

The Roles of Big Tech, Big Media, and Big Government

The British Parliament was outraged by the blatant destruction of British property, and enacted the Coercive Acts (also known as the Intolerable Acts) in 1774. The Coercive Acts closed Boston harbor to merchant shipping, established formal British military rule in Massachusetts, made British officials immune to criminal prosecution in America, and required colonists to quarter British troops. The colonists subsequently called the first Continental Congress to consider a united American resistance to the British.[8]

One of the more prominent advocates for independence from British rule was a young lawyer, Patrick Henry. He delivered fiery speeches advocating freedom from British rule and stirred the hearts of men and women that desired to be free from British taxation and laws. He delivered an eloquent speech in 1763, which set the tone for the Declaration of Independence. He proclaimed the idea of natural rights as a political theory that humans are born with certain inalienable (incapable of being surrendered) rights given to them by God their creator.

The idea of natural rights is central to the Declaration of Independence. Thomas Jefferson incorporated Patrick Henry's concepts into the preamble, *"We hold these Truths to be self-evident, that all Men are created equal, that they are endowed by their Creator with certain unalienable Rights, that among these are Life, Liberty, and the pursuit of Happiness."*

Delegates from the thirteen colonies met in the First Continental Congress to establish the rights of Americans. Shortly after the war started, the Second Continental Congress was convened in the summer of 1775 and began the process of writing the Declaration of Independence from Great Britain, which was signed on July 4, 1776. The thirteen colonies declared themselves to be independent sovereign states, no longer under British rule.

The Articles of Confederation defined our Congress as the central governing authority and remained in force until 1788. When the Articles of Confederation proved unable to meet the needs of the young nation, states sent delegates to the Constitutional Convention in Philadelphia in the summer of 1787 to draft a new, stronger governing document, creating the United States of America and its federal legislature.

Thomas Jefferson (third U.S. President) and John Adams, (second U.S. President) both sought a republic, while Thomas Paine wanted a purely representative government consisting of a one-house legislature and no executive. In contrast, Adams favored a government with a strong executive and a two-house legislature to provide a system of checks and balances. States with larger populations wanted congressional representation based on population, while smaller states demanded equal representation.[9]

Each side presented persuasive arguments, and the dispute was settled when *The Great Compromise* was forged after a heated debate.

According to the *Great Compromise*, there would be two national legislatures in Congress. Members of the House of Representatives would be allocated according to each state's population and elected by the people. In the second body—the Senate—each state would have two representatives regardless of the state's size, and state legislatures would choose Senators. This concept protected the smaller states from being dominated by the larger states. In 1913, the Seventeenth Amendment was passed, tweaking the Senate system so that Senators would be elected by the people. The Electoral College was proposed as the process for electing presidents.

The Anti-Federalists opposed the creation of a strong U.S. federal government and desired to keep more authority at the state level. They opposed the ratification of the 1787 Constitution, but our Constitution was approved by a slim margin on July 23, 1787.[10]

Due largely to the efforts of Representative James Madison, who studied the deficiencies of the Constitution pointed out by Anti-Federalists, he crafted a series of corrective proposals. Congress approved twelve articles of amendment on September 25, 1789, and submitted them to the states for ratification.

Contrary to Madison's proposal that the proposed amendments be incorporated into the main body of the Constitution, they became supplemental additions to it. They became known as the Bill of Rights amendments. <u>They added to the Constitution specific guarantees of personal freedoms and rights, clear limitations on the government's power in judicial and other proceedings, and explicit declarations that all powers not specifically granted to the federal government by the Constitution are reserved for the states, or the people.</u>[11]

Please take a minute and consider the underlined text above. Keep this in mind as you contemplate the changes enumerated in later chapters. Big Government is already usurping state and local freedoms, and if the current trend is not reversed, our Bill of Rights is in danger of being invalidated!

Here is a quote and warning from Thomas Jefferson inscribed in the Jefferson Memorial in Washington, D.C.:

> "God who gave us life, gave us liberty. Can the liberties of a nation be secure when we have removed a conviction that these liberties are the gift of God?"

Throughout America's history, Thomas Jefferson (18th century), Abraham Lincoln (19th century), and Martin Luther King, Jr. (20th century) declared the American people's freedom -- the freedom of your neighbors, your co-workers, and your children exist because we are one nation under God. Take that principle away, remove it from our national consciousness, and we will lose the very basis for the freedoms we take for granted.

Most of our founding fathers had a deep-seated belief in God. They attempted to forge a democratic republic based upon Judeo-Christian principles of shared religious texts (the Ten Commandments, incorporation of the Torah into the Christian Bible), shared moral principles (the "golden rule"), and shared cultural and historical values of Christianity and Judaism.

Both faiths affirm one God, prize the covenant between God and his people, and value the dignity of human life. The men who signed the Declaration of Independence firmly believed in these truths and knew they were risking their lives and fortunes by signing it. Nine of the 56 signers died in battle, five were captured and tortured, twelve had their homes sacked and burned, two had their sons killed, and most lost their businesses and fortunes. In addition, nearly 7,000 colonists and 24,000 British soldiers died in the war. The price of freedom was not cheap.

The United States ascended from a rag-tag collection of thirteen colonies with men and women who desired to be free of excessive taxation and oppression. They were willing to fight and die against the greatest power on earth at that time to be free. They established the Constitution and Bill of Rights that enabled the democratic Republic of the United States of America to exercise the will of "we the people" to build the most powerful nation in the world.

I believe that God acknowledged the founding principles our forefathers defined in the Constitution and Bill of Rights with this promise from the Bible:

> "*12Blessed is the nation whose God is the Lord, The people He has chosen as His own inheritance." (Psalm 33:12)*

God's blessings have been poured out upon our nation. But our nation began turning away from God. Hatred, racial discord, and lawlessness have followed. Here are three major U.S. Supreme Court decisions where they ruled to against God's principles:

- School-sponsored prayer was banned in public schools in a 1962 decision, saying that it violated the First Amendment.
- In 1973, the Roe v. Wade decision found that access to *safe and legal* abortion is a constitutional right.
- On June 26, 2015, the Court ruled all states must grant same-sex marriages and recognize same-sex marriages granted in other states.

In June 2022, the Court ruled to overturn Roe vs. Wade after 50 years. Now instead of a federal right to an abortion, this decision shifted the abortion issue to the states. It has paved the way for individual states to outright ban or permit full-term abortions. While pro-life people celebrated, the issue of access to abortion will not go away anytime soon.

The Roles of Big Tech, Big Media, and Big Government

Numerous other court decisions have been handed down affirming gay and lesbian rights. Collectively, these decisions have resulted in an ever increasing turning away from living a Godly lifestyle. As our nation continues to ignore God's laws, our nation's problems have intensified both internally with civil unrest and internationally with threats coming from China, Russia, Iran, North Korea, and international terrorists.

Today, the founding principles of our nation are being openly challenged and debated. Our nation is divided, and our union is being threatened. Northern California would like to become a separate state, and a significant number of Texans would like to secede from the union.

Today, China and Russia are powerful totalitarian nations challenging our power. Russia, China, Iran, and North Korea are waging a cyber war against us. They regularly provide support for terrorist groups. Nuclear threats are coming from Iran, North Korea, and more recently, China. Each of these nations oppresses freedom of religion and belief in God. These totalitarian nations have risen to power by trampling on the rights of their citizens while copying and stealing American innovation and technology.

Most progressives in Congress who are pushing for the United States towards socialism are attempting to change the mindset of the people to embrace socialism so control shifts to a centralized government which ultimately can have near total control over our lives.

Now it is time to review our existing capitalistic system versus socialism.

> "America was not built on fear. America was built on courage, on imagination, and an unbeatable determination to do the job at hand." – Harry S. Truman

Chapter 4

What Does the Bible Say About Capitalism, Socialism, and Government?

The Bible is silent about socialistic or capitalistic governments. It does have a lot to say about kings – both good and bad – and how people should respond to their rule.

Early Forms of Governments

Authoritarian kingdoms are described in varying degrees of detail since they were the normal form of government during most historical periods described in the Bible. In the earliest historical periods, these were the tribal heads. Some tribes grew stronger than others, or joined with them through intermarriage, and they took on the status of "king" or an equivalent title. Typically, the ruler was a man, but sometimes a woman ruled as queen. Some rulers claimed to have been selected by one or more pagan gods (some even claimed to be a "god," like the pharaohs of Egypt and the Caesars of Rome).

The rulers came to power by either separating from an existing kingdom to establish their own, overthrowing an existing kingdom, or by hereditary rights of succession. Kings or queens ruled by maintaining peace, protecting their territory from invaders, and administered justice by ensuring that the laws of the kingdom were followed.

Within a typical kingdom, the king or queen, and later in the Middle Ages, lords and nobles owned everything on their land including the peasants, crops, and village. There were exceptions where ownership of land and businesses were permitted. Some peasants were considered free and could own their own businesses like carpenters, bakers, and blacksmiths.

Even today, there are nations where the supreme leader claims to have been selected by God (or by some pagan god) and where government and religion are intertwined. Technically, these are "theocracies," but the legitimacy of the theocracy depends on the legitimacy of the underlying religion. There is only one God and Jesus Christ is the only path to the true God. Any other "theocracy" is essentially a pagan monarchy or dictatorship. Governments that claim to be theocracies exist today in Iran and Saudi Arabia.

God established a theocratic form of government for the emerging nation of Israel after its exodus from Egypt, with God as its supreme ruling authority. God gave divine guidance to His appointed leaders, who were either judges, priests, prophets, and later kings, e.g., King David and Solomon. The leaders of Israel were humans with a sin nature and their effectiveness depended on their level of obedience to God. That brought about a series of judgments on the nation. Eventually, the theocratic Jewish government disappeared and the current government of Israel is a democratic republic with a parliamentary system of government headed by a prime minister.

Early Attempts at Socialistic and Communist Principles

A group of Jews living in the Qumran caves about 100 B.C. are believed to have practiced socialism. A first century Jewish historian, Josephus described their strict and pious discipline and socialist nature:

> "Since [they are] despisers of wealth — their communal stock is astonishing — one cannot find a person among them who has more in terms of possessions... the assets of each one has been mixed together, as if they were brothers, to create one fund for all."

Some Bible theologians believe the early Christian Church, like the one described in the Acts of the Apostles, was an early form of communism and religious socialism. Their view is that communism was Christianity in practice, and Jesus was the first communist. This view was highlighted and distorted in one of Karl Marx's early writings which stated:

"Christ is the intermediary unto whom man unburdens all his divinity, all his religious bonds, so the state is the mediator unto which he transfers all his Godlessness, all his human liberty".

Peter Kropotkin, an early Russian anarchist and socialist activist, argued that the elements of mutual aid and mutual defense expressed in the medieval commune of the Middle Ages and its guild system were the same sentiments of collective self-defense apparent in modern anarchism, communism, and socialism.[12]

The early church in Jerusalem exhibited this principle:

"[32]...no one person claimed that any of their possessions was their own, but shared everything in common." (Acts 4:32)

After the brief period in the early church, the communal practices (that some characterize as socialism or communism) faded away. This approach was abandoned because it did not work when people with a sin nature were involved.

A philosophy referred to as "Christian socialism" blends some tenets of Christianity with socialism, endorsing left-wing politics and socialist economics. They interpret the Bible and the teachings of Jesus as endorsing socialism. Many Christian socialists believe capitalism to be idolatrous and rooted in the sin of greed. Christian socialists identify the cause of social inequality to be the greed that they associate with capitalism. Christian socialism became a noticeable movement in the United Kingdom beginning in 1960. The Christian Socialist Movement, known since 2013 as Christians on the Left, is one formal group and recently held less than 10% of the seats in the U.K. parliament.

European oppression of common people in the 19th Century gave rise to social justice seeker Karl Marx who wrote *The Communist Manifesto* in 1848. It became the de facto manual for multiple leaders of nations trying to initiate social changes to lift the working (proletarian) class of workers out of poverty. Some of the more prominent followers of Marx were Vladimir Lenin and Joseph Stalin in Russia, and Mao Tse-tung in China. Adolph Hitler opposed the communist party in Germany, but incorporated many elements from Marx in establishing national socialism in Germany. An estimated 100 million people worldwide have died within the last two centuries fighting for or against the adoption of socialism or communism. Millions have died from starvation, disease, torture, and imprisonment, while communist and socialist tyrants have seized and solidified their power around the world.

Marx predicted that capitalism would produce internal tensions like previous socioeconomic systems, and that those would lead to its self-destruction and replacement by a new system known as the socialist mode of production.

From Marx's ideas, *A Humanist Manifesto* was published in 1933 in the United States and signed by 34 prominent men, including philosopher and educator John Dewey. Many of the Humanist Manifesto's signers were the leading authorities in the American education system. John Dewey's reformer ideas were influential in education and social changes in the early 1900's. They taught that children should be freed from the restrictive morals and ethics of the American school system, which had been founded upon Christian ethics and moral teaching.

Unlike the later editions, the first Manifesto talked of a new "religion", and referred to Humanism as a religious movement to transcend and replace previous religions that were based on allegations of supernatural revelation. The document outlines a fifteen-point belief system. It has a secular outlook and opposes "acquisitive and profit-motivated society" while outlining a worldwide society where all people are equal and deserve equal rights and opportunities. It was to be based on voluntary cooperation.

They also denounced national sovereignty, stating a desire to see the rise of a single governing system, which would peacefully and benevolently govern the whole world. These socialist founding fathers hated free-market capitalism and desired to replace it with heavily regulated governments that controlled both production and profit-taking.

Dewey was extremely successful in transforming the educational systems in colleges and universities to teach humanism and socialistic ideals. As more and more students graduated from these universities, many adopted humanistic beliefs of rejecting God and changing our nation's moral codes. Most embraced some hybrid form of socialism. They carried these beliefs into their personal lives and work. Many became very successful, and some are now the CEO's and board members of major Fortune 500 companies. Others have become teachers in all levels of education – from pre-K to university and have openly or covertly propagated this dogma in their classrooms.

The first book of this series, *The U.S.A in Bible Prophecy Volume 1* discusses in detail most of the social and humanistic agendas under scrutiny today, e.g., Critical Race Theory, Black Lives Matter, WOKE, Antifa, and Proud Boys. These topics will be covered in this book, but with lesser detail.

It is important to note wide-scale promotion of these humanist and social views has grown steadily in public schools. Now, many teachers (and particularly the leaders of the teachers' unions), school administrators, and school boards are promoting secular humanism, and they are aided by those who write the textbooks that children use in the classroom. These views will permanently change our nation if they continue to go unchecked. As Christian taxpayers, we are paying for the demise of our own Constitution.

Charles Francis Potter was an American Unitarian minister and author. He was an original signer of the first Humanist Manifesto and honorary president of the National Education Association teacher's union. He said this about public school education:

> "Education is thus a most powerful ally of Humanism, and every American public school is a school of Humanism."

The degree of socialism in the United States government would be shocking to our founding fathers who believed more power should reside with the individual states.

Capitalism

Our Constitution recognizes private property rights, interstate commerce, and has provisions for creating the postal service, a military, and the more general provision to "provide for the general welfare" of the United States. So, you could easily argue that the U.S. was destined to become a mixture of both a capitalist and socialist nation because the Constitution clearly hints at elements we might now describe as socialism and capitalism. The U.S. today is a hybrid of both, since our government has major socialistic programs like Social Security to support the elderly and disabled. The Supplemental Nutrition Assistance Program (SNAP), commonly called food stamps, provided benefits to 42 million Americans (12.5% of the total population) in April 2023.[13]

Capitalism is an economic system where individuals or voluntary groupings of people own or control the elements of production. The four elements are investment funds, capital goods, natural resources, and labor. These are the types of capitalistic businesses: sole proprietorship, limited liability company, cooperative, partnership, and corporation.

The Constitution ensures private property rights of "citizens." Under a strict interpretation, the only one of these types of businesses receiving this type of protection under the constitution would be the sole proprietorship, but it has been interpreted more broadly.

In a series of decisions over the past 40 years, the Supreme Court has radically expanded constitutional rights for corporations. Perhaps its most impactful decision on the matter was in the 2010 Citizens United v. FEC ruling, which ruled that corporate political spending was protected speech. The effects of this decision have unleashed a wave of consequences for our republic, most notably a deluge of big money, *often called dark money*, that has drowned our ``political system. More on this will be discussed in a later chapter.

The Court's ruling was based on its assertion that corporations deserve these constitutional protections because they are nothing more than assemblies of people. However, corporations in our society function as distinct entities from the individuals that comprise them, i.e., their shareholders and employees. Therefore, corporations are not beholden to represent the opinions of those individuals. Ironically, while the First Amendment "rights" of corporations were recognized by the Supreme Court, some of these powerful corporations now seek to suppress freedom of speech for individuals who express views and opinions they disagree with.[14]

God's provisions for those in need versus the Government's socialistic programs

Many people (especially lawmakers) struggle to understand how our nation's many socialistic programs are financed. These people seem to think all the government must do is print additional money and issue more government debt. Very little consideration is given to paying it back. Let me give you a simple example of how socialism works.

Select two ten-year-old boys you know that love ice cream. On a hot summer day, tell one of the boys that you will buy him an ice cream cone to clean up the garage. Let the other boy do as he wishes (play, watch TV, take a nap). After a couple of hours of hard work, when the job is complete, summon the second boy and take both to the ice cream shop. Buy one big ice cream cone as a reward for the one that worked hard.

Then start to walk out of the ice cream shop. When the other boy demands an ice cream cone and screams, *"this is unfair"*, take the existing ice cream cone and give half to the boy screaming. Then, explain to the sobbing child whose ice cream you just stole, this is how socialism works. Government authority takes from those who have worked hard and redistributes their money to those who have not worked for it. To fully demonstrate the reality of socialist government, you should take a big bite of the ice cream before sharing it with the boy who did not do any work.

A socialistic government takes money from those who work and redistributes some of it through the social programs the government deems worthy, benefiting those who could not (or would not) provide for themselves, with a big slice of the money going to the powerful elite who run the scheme.

This concept is not what God had in mind – His plan was for the family unit to take care of needs first, and if they were too big for the family, the church would be available for assistance. Americans are

The Roles of Big Tech, Big Media, and Big Government

known for their generosity, helping those in need at home and around the world, but they prefer to provide this help voluntarily, not under government duress.

God gives instructions in the Bible to take care of those in need: the poor, widows, and orphans. Numerous Bible verses exist which give instructions on caring for those in need.

> *"[27]Pure and undefiled religion before God and the Father is this: to visit orphans and widows in their trouble, and to keep oneself unspotted from the world." (James 1:27)*

> *"[15]If a brother or sister is naked and destitute of daily food, [16]and one of you says to them, Depart in peace, be warmed and filled, but you do not give them the things which are needed for the body, what does it profit?" (James 2:15-16)*

Nowhere in the Bible does God give instructions for rulers (governments) to provide for widows and orphans. Many scriptures give instructions for citizens to pray for our rulers (elected officials), be subject to governing authorities, and pay our taxes.

> *"[1] exhort (you) first of all that supplications, prayers, intercessions, and giving of thanks be made for all men, 2 for kings and all who are in authority, that we may lead a quiet and peaceable life in all godliness and reverence." (1 Timothy 2:1)*

> *"[13]Therefore submit yourselves to every ordinance of man for the Lord's sake, whether to the king as supreme, [14]or to governors..." (1 Peter 2:13-14)*

> *"[7]Render therefore to all their due: taxes to whom taxes are due, customs to whom customs, fear to whom fear, honor to whom honor." (Romans 13:7)*

> *"[12]render unto Caesar what is Caesar's." (Mark 12:17)*

However, God gave specific instruction for the church to have provisions (money) to help the poor, widows, and orphans. God gave a command, with a challenge to prove Him wrong for anyone who obeyed it.

"¹⁰Bring all the tithes into the storehouse, That there may be food in My house, And try Me now in this, Says the Lord of hosts, If I will not open for you the windows of heaven And pour out for you such blessing That there will not be room enough to receive it." (Malachi 3:10)

A tithe is a tenth. In the Old Testament, the tithe was established to meet the financial needs of ancient Israel. For many Christians, the word tithe has come to represent any regular giving to the church, not necessarily one tenth. Christians are not under the Old Testament law, so some believe that expecting people to give 10% of their income is legalistic.

Storehouse giving is a biblical principle and guideline for Christians. But even though it would represent a norm and starting point for one's tithes and offerings, it certainly should not represent the totality of giving for any individual Christian. The opportunities and needs are too broad for any serious Christian to be that narrow and exclusive in their giving.

Failing to gain an understanding of tithing can seriously reduce the joy and security you have as a Christian. These next paragraphs reveal why the church has failed to take care of the needy and thus Big Government's role is increasing as more and more people cry out for assistance.

The following is a Gallup News article written in 2023 that is very revealing about God's decreasing role in America. These statistics reveal why more and more people are turning to the government to meet their needs instead of the church.

U.S. Church Attendance Still Lower Than Pre-Pandemic

by Jeffrey M. Jones

Story Highlights

- Church attendance down an average four points since before the pandemic
- Declines in attendance are seen among most key subgroups

- Churchgoers are mainly back in person, but 5% still attend virtually

WASHINGTON, D.C. -- U.S. church attendance has shown a small but noticeable decline compared with what it was before the COVID-19 pandemic. In the four years before the pandemic, 2016 through 2019, an average of 34% of U.S. adults said they had attended church, synagogue, mosque or temple in the past seven days. From 2020 to the present, the average has been 30%, including a 31% reading in a May 1-24 survey.

The recent church attendance levels are about 10 percentage points lower than what Gallup measured in 2012 and most prior years.

The coronavirus pandemic caused millions of Americans to avoid public gatherings, and many houses of worship were closed to help limit the spread of COVID-19. Still, Americans were able to worship remotely through services broadcast over the internet, television or radio. Most of those who reported attending religious services in 2020 said they did so virtually. Even accounting for remote attendance, however, church attendance figures were lower than in prior years.

It is not clear if the pandemic is the cause of the reduced attendance or if the decline is a continuation of trends that were already in motion. However, the temporary closure of churches and ongoing COVID-19 avoidance activities did get many Americans out of the habit of attending religious services weekly.

Church attendance is down four points among Protestants (from 44% to 40%) and seven points among Catholics (from 37% to 30%), the two largest faith groups in the U.S. Sample sizes for those in other religious groups are too small to provide reliable estimates for the period covered in this analysis.

For a nation that has *"In God We Trust"* as its motto, these are startling statistics – about 35% of Americans attend church. Satan has been very successful in weakening the church. The decline of the church can be traced to the three Supreme Court decisions that break

God's commandments previously discussed (no school prayer, abortion, same sex marriage). On top of these decisions, add an educational system that is increasingly pro-humanist and anti-Christian so it easy to understand why the important role of the Church is being weakened.

It is impossible for the existing church to fully meet the demands of the needy at present if giving continues at its current rate. The inability of the church to meet its God designed role to help the needy has left the door wide-open for the government to attempt to meet these needs. People are crying out to the members of Congress, "give me more social benefits!"

<u>Even if the current efforts to move our country towards a democratic nation are not immediately successful, a base of future support is being built that will continue attempting to erode resistance to the proposed socialistic programs.</u>

Before proceeding, here is a high-level view on the hydra of Big Tech, Big Media, and Big Government and their interconnections.

The mythical hydra's necks were connected to one body, sharing its heart, blood flow, and vital organs. Its legs carried the beast's necks and heads to a single destination. Similarly, the heads of the Big Tech, Big Media and Big Government hydra are connected and they are all moving together with one destination in mind.

The leaders (and most of the underlings) of the three liberal *"Bigs"* generally share the same beliefs and values, preached by the left-leaning education system and "elite" social circles. Key personnel often flow from one *"Big"* to another *"Big."* Big Government people move to Big Media, e.g., George Stephanopoulos to ABC via the Obama administration. Big Tech people move to Big Government, e.g., President Biden's White House staff has 13 aides - some of them with the ear of the president - have previously worked for Google, Amazon, Apple, Facebook (META), Lyft, Microsoft, Twitter, or Uber[15].

Similarly, big money flows freely from one Big to another. Politicians in Big Government and their Super PACs spend huge sums of money (billions of dollars) to buy political advertising from Big Tech and Big

Media. Big Tech and Big Media returns these favors by giving campaign donations to politicians in Big Government. Then to acknowledge their donations, the politicians in Big Government awards Big Tech and Big Media lucrative contracts for their services.

"Big" does not adequately describe the enormity of Big Tech, Big Media, and Big Government. While we observe the "public faces" for each hydra head, much of their work is done by hordes of faceless technocrats, bureaucrats, minions, and computer algorithms. The "Big" corporations are among the world's largest and there is a high degree of overlap in ownership. For example, cable service provider Comcast owns NBC and MSNBC. Amazon's Jeff Bezos owns the Washington Times newspaper. The Wall Street Journal and Fox News have the same ownership.

Big Tech is generally portrayed in today's news and in Congressional hearings as meaning Google, Amazon, Twitter, and Facebook (META) (the Big Four). Often the media also includes Apple and Microsoft with Big Tech because of their influence and the massive amount of personal data they collect.

The Big Four are in the news because their online platforms are being used to shape opinions on current news, influence voter decisions prior to elections, and suppress opinions they disagree with.

These companies have become so sophisticated they know what kind of ads to display as *clickbait* while you are using their "free" services. They can also suspend your online account if you post something they believe is fraudulent, or inconsistent with their views and objectives. They may flag something as "hate speech," even if it is just a statement of fact with no malevolence at all.

The boundaries between Big Tech and Big Media overlap in the creation and distribution of news and in their political influence.

In this book, the definition of Big Tech includes the Big Four plus Apple and Microsoft because they collect massive amounts of your personal data. In addition to the six Big Tech corporations, there are *big tech* corporations that are key to End Times that develop technological innovations in hardware, software, and cloud computing services, e.g., Intel, Cisco, Dell, IBM, HP, SAP, Amazon Web Services, and Oracle.

Big Media refers to newspapers (and magazines), radio, television, and motion pictures. As previously explained, these groups overlap into this space as communication mediums because of their ability to spread news, affect personal political opinions, and promote political paid advertisements at unprecedented speeds while collecting massive amounts of personal data.

Big Government describes a government intent on expanding existing social services and the creation of new ones for American citizens. It wants to radically change the lives of Americans "for their own good." For example, it wants citizens to follow specific medical practices, purchase certain goods (like electric vehicles) and services ("green" energy) and absorb certain information and beliefs, while restricting the other choices available for Americans. To do this, Big Government will exercise increased control over our economy and personal lives.

A frequent question from believers is *"what should we be looking for before the Rapture? Will it be signs of wars, famines, pestilences, or earthquakes?"*

My answer surprises them as it probably will you. My response is *"look at the ever-increasing capability of technology because it is a major enabler."* A detailed analysis of Daniel's prophecy at the *"...time of the end...knowledge shall increase"* (Daniel 12:4) will be presented depicting just how fast technology has increased, but more importantly how much faster it will develop in the next few years.

Beginning in early 2023, the news media began broadcasting how Artificial Intelligence (AI) was rapidly developing and would soon be smarter than humans. The news media daily broadcast that AI could eliminate millions of skilled jobs.

Some *AI visionaries* were quoted as believing we humans could come under the control of AI robots. Robots, with AI inside a human-like form, could be made to do remarkable things. But they could be told to do horrible things like steal and commit cyber-crimes. For example, a command could be issued to hack John Doe's bank account and transfer the funds elsewhere. AI technology has already been used to create fake videos and audio recordings that could be used for malicious reasons. AI could create a world in which "no one knows what is true anymore."

These advancements will provide the needed developments the Antichrist requires to implement his one-world government and one-world religion.

Many people find these developments enlightening and scary because if they watch the news or read the newspaper, they see these events beginning to unfold before them.

Now, let us examine how inconspicuously Big Tech began.

Here is a quote for you to ponder as you read about Big Tech.

> "It has become appallingly obvious that our technology has exceeded our humanity." – Attributed to Albert Einstein

Chapter 5

Big Tech: The Beginning

Storms that develop into a hurricane have a modest beginning. Off the west coast of Africa, just north of the equator, a thunderstorm forms. It can be just a typical towering thunderstorm cloud, but it might grow into something quite different – a hurricane - if the thunderstorm clouds begin to rotate around an area of low atmospheric pressure called a tropical depression. If enough energy from the warmth of the tropical ocean water can be acquired, these circling thunderstorms can grow into a single tropical storm. There is a continuous supply of energy as it moves across the warm waters of the Atlantic Ocean, and the warm, moist air then causes the storm to grow into a hurricane.

The metaphorical *Perfect Political Storm* attacking the United States has a beginning element – Big Tech. The Bible tells us that Satan will attempt to control the world by requiring everyone to take the famous mark of the beast, 666. Most Christians give little thought to how he will control all commerce, or how he will prevent those who refuse to take the mark from buying and selling.

To accomplish this globally, Satan needs massive supercomputer systems with unprecedented amounts of data storage capacity running over networks faster than any we currently have today. He needs communication technologies capable of simultaneously communicating with billions of people before he can implement a one-world government.

Satan needs people to enhance the existing surveillance capabilities, create new quantum computer systems along with the sophisticated Artificial Intelligence (AI) software is needed to efficiently process massive amounts of data and to enable near instantaneous retrieval of this data. The Antichrist needs social media to effectively communicate with billions of people worldwide. Big Tech will provide these resources through enhancements to existing systems and creation of new devices to enable the Antichrist to run the new one-world order.

What does the Bible say about the advancement of knowledge in End Times?

Over 2,500 years ago, God told the prophet Daniel:

> *"⁴But you, Daniel, shut up the words, and seal the book until the time of the end; many shall run to and fro, and knowledge shall increase." (Daniel 12:4)*

Like many Bible verses, different translations exist with subtle differences in meaning.

The *GOD'S WORD* translation:

> *"⁴But you, Daniel, keep these words secret, and seal the book until the end times. Many will travel everywhere, and knowledge will grow."*

The Living Bible translation:

> *"⁴But Daniel, keep this prophecy a secret; seal it up so that it will not be understood until the end times, when travel and education shall be vastly increased."*

My belief is each translation has a valid meaning as the End Times approach.

One interpretation of the phrase, *"many shall run to and fro, and knowledge shall increase,"* refers to the travel in the End Times with cars, buses, trains, and airplanes, as well as the increase of knowledge. The increase in knowledge can be attributed to electronic communications using digital communications applications like META and Twitter and mankind's fast access to massive information databases through the internet.

The increase in knowledge applies to science and technology, but also encompasses the increase in knowledge and understanding of Bible prophecies. Before the End Times began with the rebirth of the nation of Israel in 1948, it was impossible to understand how many End Times prophecies might be fulfilled, e.g., those that applied to

Israel could not possibly be fulfilled since Israel as a nation had not existed for nineteen centuries.

Other commentaries and Bible renditions convey the thought that the reference in Daniel 12:4 is not to travel and to gain physical knowledge, but describes how people will search the Scriptures to gain spiritual knowledge. The thought is that people—the wise—will go to and fro in the Scriptures, searching them daily to see whether the recorded things are true (compare Acts 17:11), and thereby increasing in godly knowledge (2 Peter 3:18).

There is still a third way in which the phrase in Daniel 12:4 has been rendered and understood. The revised Luther Bible of 2017 translates:

> *"4Many will wander around (in the sense of, walking around in error, "herumirren" in German), and wickedness will increase."*[16]

To demonstrate the speed of current technological advancements, let's examine the history of travel. Beginning around 4,000 B.C. animal-drawn wheeled vehicles were developed in the Ancient Near East. Only in the early 1900's did motorized vehicles begin to change the way people traveled. No significant advances occurred for nearly 6,000 years!

Here is a brief history of rapid advancements in transportation that have occurred in the last two hundred years.

- Modern rail transport systems using steam locomotives first appeared in England in the 1820s.
- The development of motorized cars started in 1886 in Germany, and in the U.S. in 1908 with the production of Ford's first Model T.
- The Wright brothers made the first sustained, controlled and powered heavier-than-air flight on December 17, 1903.
- The first human spaceflight was achieved by the Soviet space program in 1961.

- The first spaceflight to the Moon was NASA's Apollo 11 mission in 1969.[17]
- The first self-sufficient and truly self-driving cars appeared in the 1980s.[18]

For thousands of years, advancement in travel and the knowledge to build the machines that made these advances possible simply did not exist. In the early 1900's it was widely believed that manned flight was impossible, but jet airplanes now routinely travel near the speed of sound carrying passengers around the world. Billionaires are working to establish commercial rocket travel and wealthy people are booking future flights to the moon through Virgin Galactic.

These travel advancements are trivial when compared to advances in information technology (IT) – computers, data storage, and networks. Future phenomenal advancements in IT are being tested today that will expand IT capabilities dramatically.

What is driving the need for technology to advance?

First, there is big money to be made selling advanced technology to corporations and the government. Second, advancement is essential in Satan's plans. Satan needs ready-made applications that can quickly and seamlessly be adapted for him to achieve his attempt to control the world.

When the Rapture occurs, estimates range from one-eighth of the world's population and as high as one-third of the U.S. population will ascend to heaven. These people will vanish in a "twinkling of an eye." Key Christian people in technology, business, and the government will suddenly vanish from the earth. So many key people will disappear that the Antichrist will have to rely on the remaining people and existing data systems to establish his one-world government.

Development of new capabilities will become very difficult after the Rapture with fewer people to do the programming. Further, the IT people left behind after the Rapture will face so many day-to-day challenges, e.g., crime, famine, war, disease, and natural disasters that will severely impact their ability to work.

As we explore the rapid development of IT, it will be readily apparent these advancements are fulfilling the prophecy in Daniel pertaining to the increase and advancement of knowledge.

Tim Berners-Lee, a British scientist, invented the World Wide Web (WWW) in 1989. (Sorry, please don't be deceived, Al Gore did not "invent the internet" as he once implied.) The web was originally conceived and developed to meet the demand for automated information sharing between scientists in universities and institutes around the world. In 2021, about 1.8 billion websites exist and hundreds are added daily.

Internet access is readily available in the richer nations of the world, where the communications networks have been established and people own the smart phones, computers, and other devices for web access. Though the poorer nations of the Third World are relatively disadvantaged, there is still widespread availability because the new wireless technologies, improved rechargeable batteries, solar power and satellite technologies facilitate this access even in places that lack a sound electrical grid and wired or fiber optics data communications. Expect Satan to work toward reaching everyone in the world through these means.

A new internet is evolving: the Internet of Things (IoT). The IoT describes physical objects (or groups of such objects), that are embedded with sensors, processing ability, software, and other technologies that connect and exchange data with other devices and systems over the Internet or other communications networks.

IoT has evolved due to the convergence of multiple technologies, including ubiquitous (present at the same time and everywhere) computing, commodity sensors, increasingly powerful embedded systems, and machine learning. Since more and more relevant data is stored on the internet, this new data will speed up computer learning as AI matures. The exponential amount of new data being added daily enhances AI decision making. Think of how humans learn – new information and experiences fill our brain with more information to make better decisions.[19]

The Mark of the Beast - 666

The knowledge explosion is the most dramatic sign we have that the End Times are near, yet most people do not recognize its importance.

The Bible says a time will come when the Antichrist is in power, that to buy and sell anything you must receive a mark on the right hand or the forehead – commonly called the mark of the beast. Those without the mark will not be able to buy or sell anything.

> "[16]He causes all, both small and great, rich and poor, free and slave, to receive a mark on their right hand or on their foreheads, [17]and that no one may buy or sell except one who has the mark or the name of the beast, or the number of his name. [18]Here is wisdom. Let him who has understanding calculate the number of the beast, for it is the number of a man: His number is 666." (Revelation 13:16-18)

After the Rapture, the Antichrist will take control of the best-of-the-best business and government systems so he has immediate access to existing citizen's profiles worldwide.

By this time, AI will have advanced to the point whenever a person goes to buy and sell, they will be forced to identify themselves. If their name is not in the database as having taken the mark, their name will be automatically entered as a rebel that has not taken the mark. They will be unable to buy or sell, but will receive immense persecution to take the mark of the beast or face death.

For centuries, people have wondered how the mark will be applied and how will buying and selling be controlled. Internet-based companies like Amazon, Google, META, Twitter, and TikTok have profiled you to a level never before possible. They know where you live and have your personal information. They know your preferences and everything you buy online. Ultimately, the Antichrist will use your personal information to control buying and selling.

Big Tech companies gather your personal information for marketing purposes to sell you more products. Big businesses create the demand for Big Tech to continue advancing technology to provide better and faster access to your data. When you are browsing online, seconds matter and if the retrieval of your data takes too long, you have already moved on before you can see the tempting ad designed for you.

People access the internet by using either a tablet, computer, or cell phone. Mass production has made these devices affordable to almost everyone. Today's cell phones not only can store lots of digital data, they can take photos, record conversations, and they have a GPS tracking system for navigation using a maps application. You can also be tracked if you are carrying the cell phone.

As you surf the net, Big Tech is constantly capturing data about you. Those in control of the storage and delivery platforms can hide or prevent access to information. They also can control what they want you to see.

The mark of the beast is a fascinating (and scary) subject to many people. It is implied in the Bible that not everyone – Christians and non-Christians will take the mark. It is understandable why a Christian would refuse to take the mark because a true Christian will not renounce their belief in Jesus. Why non-Christians would refuse to take the mark was puzzling to me until the COVID-19 vaccine became available.

As of May 2023, the lack of public enthusiasm for COVID-19 vaccines was revealed in a Pew Research Poll that revealed only about a third of U.S. adults have the highest level of available protection against the coronavirus.[20] This is an astounding finding in lieu of the fact the vaccine is free, proclaimed to be safe, and could save your life. Vaccinations began in December 2020. Federal targets for vaccinations for the total population lagged behind expectations. To get the non-vaxxed people to take the vaccine, gut-wrenching emotional pleas on television and social media depicted non-vaxxed people as being a dangerous threat to others and even being responsible for killing those who could catch COVID-19 from them.

However, many people refused to get the "jab." Some cite various reasons, e.g., existing immunity from a prior COVID-19 infection, worries about adverse reactions to the vaccine, severe health problems from prior immunizations, and other underlying medical conditions. Some cite religious objections. Other people don't object to the vaccine, per se, but object to the totalitarian approach forcing mandatory vaccinations.

Some people referred to the doctors and health officials calling for mandatory vaccines as "needle Nazis."[21] "Proof of vaccination" became increasingly problematic because it was demanded in order to work, travel, and enter some venues like movie theaters or restaurants.

As vaccines became more readily available throughout the country in 2021, the conversation about work vaccine mandates heated up. In early November of that year, the U.S. Department of Labor and the Occupational Safety and Health Administration (OSHA) announced an emergency temporary COVID standard for safety in the workplace, stating that employers with more than 100 employees "must develop, implement and enforce a mandatory COVID-19 vaccination policy," unless they adopt a policy requiring employees to choose to either be vaccinated or undergo regular COVID-19 testing and wear a face covering at work. Although the intended measure to protect U.S. workers, the policy was met with backlash.

The Supreme Court blocked most of the policy soon after it went into effect, though it allowed the mandate to stand for medical facilities that take Medicare or Medicaid payments. The Court argued that regulating public health more broadly to private businesses was outside of the scope of OSHA, whose mandate would have required 84 million Americans to be vaccinated.

Companies adjusted their vaccine mandates throughout 2022. While some companies choose to keep vaccination requirements in place, others began to repeal them as soon as possible. Though the workforce seems to be moving forward without the COVID-19 measures it once had, the virus has not gone away.[22]

Now, we can understand that when the Antichrist demands a mark be placed in the right hand or forehead, millions of people will resist, but do so at the risk of severe punishment or death. Then a black market will spring up for food. It will be chaos.

The Antichrist will nationalize, or otherwise take control of online purchases from the most efficient and reliable suppliers, absorbing or replacing leaders in online sales in the United States and worldwide. At first, the changes will seem minor from the perspective of the online customer. For instance, after logging into your online account, you enter your unique 16-digit ID number assigned by the Antichrist. A computer mounted camera would transmit an image of you to be analyzed using facial recognition to identify you and to verify you have the mark.

Online purchasing accounts for less than 20% of buying in 2023, but that is growing. Customers can be pushed online with cheaper pricing, product availability, security threats, and pandemic fears. Smaller businesses are being forced out of business in favor of big retailers. Most big retailers combine online buying services with their physical storefronts and warehouses. It will be easy to force people toward these channels in the tumultuous Tribulation period.

How will the mark of the beast be verified at brick-and-mortar stores?

New technologies have driven endless speculation about what the physical mark will be for buying and selling. Some think it will be an implantable microchip. Others think it will be a visible 666 tattoo. Still others think it will involve barcodes, QR codes, social security numbers, or RFID chips.

After witnessing the fierce resistance many people have to taking the COVID-19 vaccines, whatever the mark turns out to be, it will have to be visible, quick to apply, and relatively painless. Unlike the requests being made to get out of taking COVID-19 vaccines, no exceptions will be granted - regardless of how it impairs your looks or how your body may react to it.

Since the mark is supposed to be visible, one of the plausible techniques would be a form of tattooing called micropigmentation that is commonly used to color eyelashes, eyelids, and lips. Micropigmentation is not technically considered a tattoo. Tattoo ink goes much deeper into the skin and is injected with a thicker needle and is more painful. One quick micropigmentation session using a specialized device could administer the 666 mark with a unique identifying marker.

Since people age and skin wrinkles, another possibility is the mark will be used in connection with a cell phone using something like the current Apple Pay cell phone app. The mark will be verified visually using the camera on your phone or PC, and then you will use either device to buy and sell. No development is necessary!

A digital currency like bitcoins will replace physical money. It may surprise you to learn that many U.S. companies accept bitcoins for payments today: Microsoft, Overstock, Home Depot, NameCheap, Starbucks, Whole Foods, NewEgg, Tesla, and Lolli. Visa, Mastercard, Square, and PayPal accept various forms of crypto payments.

What is a Central Bank Digital Currency (CBDC)?

A CBDC is virtual money backed and issued by a central bank. As bitcoins, cryptocurrencies, and stablecoins have become more popular, the world's central banks have realized that they need to provide an alternative—or let the future of money pass them by.

In 1993, the Bank of Finland launched the Avant smart card, an electronic form of cash. Although the system was eventually dropped in the early 2000s, it can be considered the world's first CBDC.[23]

As technology advanced, the desire to move to a digital currency has increased dramatically. The following is a summary of how fast the world governments are moving to a digital economy from the Atlantic Council Geoeconomics Center.

> There are many reasons to explore digital currencies, and the motivation of different countries for issuing CBDCs depends on their economic situation. CBDCs will provide easy and safer access to money for unbanked and underbanked populations plus they introduce competition and resilience in the domestic payments market. Increased competition leads to incentives to provide cheaper and better access to money by increasing efficiency in payments and lowering transaction costs. This, in turn creates programmable money and improves transparency in money flows.

New payments systems create externalities that impact the daily lives of citizens, and can jeopardize the national security objectives of the country. They can, for example, limit the United States' ability to track cross-border flows and enforce sanctions. In the long term, the absence of U.S. leadership and standards setting can have geopolitical consequences, especially if China and other countries maintain their first-mover advantage in the development of CBDCs.

- 19 of the G20 countries are now in the advanced stage of CBDC development. Of those, 9 countries are already in pilot. Nearly every G20 country has made significant progress and invested new resources in these projects over the past six months.
- 11 countries have fully launched a digital currency. China's 2023 pilot is being used by 260 million people.[24]

The United States is developing a central bank digital currency. The Federal Reserve has not made a decision on issuing a central bank digital currency (CBDC) as of July 12, 2023 and can only proceed with an authorizing law.[25]

It is inevitable our currency system in the U.S. will move to a digital one. Many stores accepted only credit cards during the peak of the COVID-19 pandemics in 2020. Do you remember the penny shortage? Even now, stores and coin-operated devices (vending machines and laundromats) complain about coin shortages. Look for legislatures to authorize a move to a digital currency on a national basis.

Multiple alternatives exist to verify the mark of the beast. Barcodes, code scanners and RFID chips and microchips are among them. We have been putting microchips in our pets for years, so why not humans? The animal chips are passive, so they do not emit tracking signals. When technology advances enough to reduce the size of transmitters, GPS tracking capability could be added to insertable chips for humans, containing all your personal data like credit cards, bank account, health conditions, etc. Plus, your every movement could be tracked.

How far away from human insertable chips are we today? It is closer than you probably realize.

The following article describes the development of human implantable microchips.

Tiny injectable chips use ultrasound for monitoring

Researchers at Columbia Engineering report that they have built what they say is the world's smallest single-chip system, consuming a total volume of less than 0.1 mm. The system is as small as a dust mite and visible only under a microscope. To achieve this, the team used ultrasound to both power and communicate with the device wirelessly.

Widely used to monitor and map biological signals, to support and enhance physiological functions, and to treat diseases, implantable medical devices are transforming healthcare and improving the quality of life for millions of people. Researchers are increasingly interested in designing wireless, miniaturized implantable devices. These devices could be used to monitor physiological conditions, such as temperature, blood pressure, glucose, and respiration for both diagnostic and therapeutic procedures.

"We wanted to see how far we could push the limits on how small a functioning chip we could make," said the study's leader Ken Shepard, Lau Family professor of electrical engineering and professor of biomedical engineering. "This is a new idea of 'chip as system'—this is a chip that alone, with nothing else, is a completely functioning electronic system. This should be revolutionary for developing wireless, miniaturized implantable medical devices that can sense different things, be used in clinical applications, and eventually approved for human use."[26]

Microsoft is working on smart tattoos.

The following is a verbatim quote from the Microsoft research web page. Could this technology be used for the "mark?"

These interactive tattoos are capacitive and can send signals to any device via touch. They can be laser cut into custom shapes, applied to almost any surface, then connected to a device via Bluetooth from a microprocessor. While the tattoos are temporary, especially on the skin, they can last for months on non-skin surfaces, including fabrics or 3D prints (researchers are also exploring their use on prosthetics). Microsoft researchers recently partnered with the Microsoft Garage team over the Summer of 2018 to host a "Hack-a-Tatt" workshop that enabled employees to design and build their own on-body controls.

A similar method is the use of quantum dot tattoos that are tagged with fluoresce, so the information will glow under UV light after they're injected. Rice University is working with The Bill and Melinda Gates Foundation, so these "become something like a barcode tattoo." At present, they are limited to vaccines, but could easily be expanded to include more information.

If you like pursuing conspiracy theories, Google "Bill Gates conspiracy theories." They abound.

The needs of science are driving the development of human implantable microchips. Will they be perfected in time for the Antichrist to use them? If not, there are other solutions readily available.

Facial recognition and other AI advancements for use in End Times

Satan's desire for control is insatiable. He wants total control.

He will implement tools (many of which are being implemented in the U.S. presently) to control borders, airlines, airports, transport hubs, stadiums, mega events, concerts, conferences, etc.

Biometrics are playing an important and growing role in real-time crime detection and other commercial applications. Facial, iris and voice recognition, finger and palm print identification, and ear acoustic authentication are maturing biometrics techniques being used today. These applications, which use AI and data analytics, are rapidly becoming commonplace across the world.

The Roles of Big Tech, Big Media, and Big Government

Facial recognition can often prove one of the best biometrics because images can be taken without touching or interacting with the individual being identified, and those images are recorded and instantly checked against existing databases.

Before proceeding with further validation of Daniel's incredible prophecy with descriptions of the soon coming astounding and almost unbelievable advancements to information technology by Big Tech, here is a short overview of the development of the computer, disk storage, and software. Please note the first commercial computer was delivered in 1946. After the nation of Israel was created by the United Nations in 1948, the advancements keep coming faster and faster with phenomenal new capabilities.

Here are some key milestones.

- 1936: Alan Turing develops the concept for the modern computer.

- 1937: J.V. Atanasoff, a professor of physics and mathematics at Iowa State University, attempts to build the first computer without gears, cams, belts, or shafts.

- 1946: Mauchly and Presper build UNIVAC, the first commercial computer for business and government applications.

- 1953: Grace Hopper develops the first computer language, which eventually becomes known as COBOL.

- 1964: Douglas Engelbart shows a prototype of the modern personal computer, with a mouse and a graphical user interface (GUI). This marks the evolution of the computer from a specialized machine for scientists and mathematicians to technology that is more accessible to the general public.

- 1965: MIT as part of its Compatible Time-Sharing System introduces email.

- 1969: The ARPAnet is the first large-scale, general-purpose computer network to connect different kinds of computers together.

- 1971: Alan Shugart leads a team of IBM engineers who invent the "floppy disk," allowing data to be shared among computers.
- 1975: Two "computer geeks," Paul Allen and Bill Gates, wrote software for the Altair, using the new BASIC language. On April 4, 1975 they formed their own software company, Microsoft.
- 1974-1977: Several personal computers hit the market, including the Altair, IBM 5100, Radio Shack's TRS-80 (affectionately known as the "Trash 80"), and the Commodore PET.
- 1978: Accountants rejoice at the introduction of VisiCalc, the first computerized spreadsheet program.
- 1979: Word processing becomes a reality as MicroPro International releases WordStar.
- 1985: Microsoft announces Windows.
- 1996: The Google search engine is released.
- 2004: Facebook is launched.
- 2005: YouTube, a video sharing service, is founded.
- 2006: Twitter is launched.
- 2007: The iPhone brings many computer functions to the smartphone.
- 2012: Facebook gains 1 billion users on October 4, 2012.
- 2015: Apple releases the Apple Watch.
- 2016: The first re-programmable quantum computer was created.[27]

If you examine the last twenty-five years, both the method of doing business and our personal lives have experienced revolutionary changes. Never in history have so many dramatic changes occurred so fast. Daniel's prophecy of increasing knowledge is unfolding before

The Roles of Big Tech, Big Media, and Big Government

us. The exponential growth of technology is a sign - a sign the End Times are arriving at our doorstep.

However great this advancement may seem, the introduction of quantum technology will increase current digital supercomputers capabilities by factors of 10, 100, or 1,000. With these enhanced capacities, AI will continue to advance at breathtaking speeds.

Implementation of quantum capabilities to replace supercomputers and existing networks will make Satan's plans possible.

Should you worry about what the future of Big Tech will bring?

"We're changing the world with technology." - Bill Gates

Are you feeling overwhelmed?

"[2]... I will cry to You, When my heart is overwhelmed; Lead me to the rock that is higher than I." (Psalm 61:2)

As a believer our future lies in the HOPE in the rock of our salvation – Jesus – and not in any of the "*Bigs.*"

Chapter 6

Big Tech: The Future

This discussion contains technical jargon, so only a brief summary is given, but if you're interested in the details, check out the sources in the footnotes.

This discussion is significant for two reasons.

1. The rapid growth in technology is a significant sign that we are extremely near to the End Times events, which means we could expect the Rapture soon.
2. Big Tech will play a major role to provide the Antichrist the tools needed to attempt to control mankind.

These developments are somewhat creepy (even a bit scary) and you may wish that someone would stop them. Some are speculative and may not occur. Please keep in mind that God is in control and He is fully aware of the current situation and all future developments. His plan calls for Satan, sin, and death to be vanquished and all believers in Jesus will be saved for an eternal life of peace and joy.

Here's an explanation of quantum technology and how it exponentially increases computing power.

Why do we need quantum computers?

When scientists and engineers encounter difficult problems, they turn to supercomputers. These are very large classical supercomputers, often with thousands of classical central processing cores capable of running very large calculations and advanced artificial intelligence. However, supercomputers are binary code-based machines reliant on 20th-century transistor technology. They struggle to solve certain kinds of problems.

If a supercomputer gets stumped, that's probably because the big classical machine was asked to solve a problem with a high degree of complexity. When classical computers fail, it's often due to complexity.

Complex problems are problems with lots of variables interacting in complicated ways. Modeling the behavior of individual atoms in a molecule is a complex problem, because of all the different electrons interacting with one another. Identifying subtle patterns of fraud in financial transactions or new physics in a supercollider are also complex problems. There are some complex problems that we do not know how to solve with classical computers on any scale.

The real world runs on quantum physics. Computers that make calculations using the quantum states of quantum bits should in many situations be our best tools for understanding it.

A quantum processor is a wafer not much bigger than the one found in a laptop. And a quantum hardware system is about the size of a car, made up mostly of cooling systems to keep the superconducting processor at its ultra-cold operational temperature.

A classical computer processor uses classical bits to perform its operations. A quantum computer uses qubits (CUE-bits) to run multidimensional quantum algorithms.

The opportunity for quantum computing to solve large scale combinatorics problems faster and cheaper has encouraged billions of dollars of investment in recent years.[28]

Artificial Intelligence is changing our world, only we don't realize how deeply it is already embedded in computer systems' software.

There are four different types of AI software for quantum computers:

1. Artificial Intelligence Platforms: This will provide the platform for developing an application from scratch. Many built-in algorithms are provided in this. Drag and drop facility makes it easy to use.

2. Chatbots: This software will give the effect that a human or person is participating in a conversation.

3. Deep Learning Software: It includes speech recognition, image recognition etc.

4. Machine Learning Software: Machine learning is the technique which will make the computer learn through data.

The applications from these types of software are virtually unlimited. They are increasingly being used by businesses and will continue to mature.[29]

Have you ever bought a new computer thinking you would have faster internet transactions, but be disappointed to find out your internet connection was too slow? Following is a brief description describing how network speeds will have to increase to meet the demands of quantum computers. Forget about the claims that 5G networks are 20 times faster than current networks – that is not fast enough to prevent quantum computer generated data bottlenecks.

Quantum Networks

The evolving quantum computers will generate so much more data that existing networks will be overwhelmed. Quantum networks and quantum computing are related. Both leverage quantum physics: the entanglement between particles that enables them to share states -- or in the digital sense, information.

Quantum networking will not only deliver increases in speed, but they will establish secure connections between digital devices (including the conventional variety - yours and mine) using a physics technique that would be permanently crack-proof. It would rather let the connection crash than allow it to be pilfered.[30]

Quantum's networking capabilities will include wireless transmission. Wireless is a unique digital transmission technology using wireless transmitters and receivers instead of in-ground fiber or cables. Cell phones almost exclusively use wireless transmissions.

Data Storage

The Roles of Big Tech, Big Media, and Big Government

The last component The Antichrist needs for Big Tech to advance is data storage. Quantum computing generates massive quantities of data that must be stored. Today's simple concept of daisy chaining together disk arrays will not be economically practicable, or fast enough to supply the desired response times quantum computers need.

Here are two of the major evolving technologies being studied to solve the capacity problem quantum computing creates.

> DNA storage is one of the most futuristic technologies of data storage. This concept allows the system to store data in DNA nucleotides. Microsoft Research has developed a fully automated system for writing, storing, and reading data encoded in DNA. Several companies are working to advance DNA storage technology.

> Crystal technology, also called 5D storage, seeks to store data in infinitesimally small and long-lasting glass structures. These crystals are made with lasers that encode data in microscopic structures of the glass surfaces. The five dimensions of quartz are utilized resulting in a huge amount of data that can be stored in these crystals. For its capacity, this type of emerging technology is also known as "5D tech." This is an evolving development and unproven at present.[31]

Before closing the discussion on Big Tech of the future, another concept, *singularity,* needs to be introduced because it graphically illustrates that knowledge is increasing exponentially in the End Times. Singularity plays a frightening role in the evolving use of AI by Big Tech, and some experts believe it could *threaten* the human race.

Do you ever read or watch fictional dystopian books or movies where computers using AI are programmed to continue to learn beyond the capabilities they were programmed for? The result is a battle for control between man and machine. Humanity continues to learn more and more about our universe, and the same analogy can be applied to AI as it learns about technological advancements. Humans are seeking to take control from God of their destinies.

"²¹There are many plans in a man's heart, Nevertheless the Lord's counsel—that will stand." (Proverbs 19:21)

If you are still a skeptic and think that the rapid increase in technology is not an End Times sign, this next discussion is for you.

Singularity

Did you watch *"The Terminator,"* the 1984 movie starring Arnold Schwarzenegger, or read the 2011 novel *"Robopocalypse,"* by Daniel Wilson? If so, the following discussion describes the prime premise behind those science fiction tales. "Singularity" is the term used by scientists and sociologists for this theoretical premise and is explained below.

> Technological singularity is a hypothetical point in time at which technological growth becomes uncontrollable and irreversible, resulting in unforeseeable changes to human civilization. According to the most popular version of the singularity hypothesis, called intelligence explosion, an upgradable intelligent agent will eventually enter a "runaway reaction" of self-improvement cycles, each new and more intelligent generation appearing more and more rapidly, causing an "explosion" in intelligence, and resulting in a powerful superintelligence that qualitatively far surpasses all human intelligence.[32]

Some *AI visionaries* were quoted as believing we humans could come under the control of AI robots. Robots, with AI inside a human-like form, could be made to do remarkable things. But they could be told to do horrible things like steal and commit cyber-crimes. For example, a command could be issued to hack John Doe's bank account and transfer the funds elsewhere. AI technology has already been used to create fake videos and audio recordings that could be used for malicious reasons. AI could create a world in which "no one knows what is true anymore."

Over 1,100 developers and scientists signed an open letter dated March 28, 2023 that called on "all AI labs to immediately pause for at least 6 months the training of AI systems." Eye-opening statements in the letter ask, "Should we develop nonhuman minds that might eventually outnumber, outsmart, obsolete, and replace us? And, should we risk loss of control of our civilization?"[33]

My condensed and simple definition of singularity is that technological change that becomes so rapid that humans can no longer keep up. Humanity will need an AI system to continuously update and manage evolving technology.

Buckminster Fuller in 2013 created the *"Knowledge Doubling Curve,"* and his studies determined that until 1900 human knowledge doubled approximately every century. By the end of World War II knowledge was doubling every 25 years. According to IBM, the build-out of the "internet of things" will lead to the doubling of knowledge every 12 hours.[34]

My head hurts trying to comprehend this. Here is the takeaway for you: computers can store and make more complex decisions to process huge amounts of factual (or non-factual) data than the human brain. AI is designed to process huge amounts of data to achieve the desired results. As more data is factored into the AI decision process, the result is (theoretically) better and better decisions.

But the definition of "better" begins with the meaning of "good." "Better" decisions from the perspectives of sinful man and Satan's world system will likely bear little similarity to what our holy God calls "good."

Technologies that drive AI advancements are being enhanced at ever-increasing rates of development. *"Big"* is only going to get bigger, faster, and more reliable. People wonder, "why." The answer is simple. *"Big"* companies will commit the financial resources to pay for the developments so they can enhance their operating efficiencies to improve their profit margins. The almighty dollar drives technology developments to advance faster and more efficiently!

Here is another method of explaining singularity through automation.

Automation of Automation

The following explanation explains why many scientists fear AI.

AI is a watershed moment for the world. Humans' fundamental technology is our intelligence. We're in the process of automating artificial intelligence so that we can augment ours. AI is software that writes itself, and it writes software that no humans can. It's incredibly complex. And we can automate intelligence to operate at the speed of light, and because of computers, we can automate intelligence and scale it out globally instantaneously.

Today we have this new technology called AI that can write complex software so that we can automate it. The whole goal of writing software is to automate something. We are in this new world where, over the next 10 years, we are going to see the *automation of automation*.

Recommender systems are the most important AI system today which is the most important machine-learning pipeline in the world today. It is the engine for search ads, online shopping, music, books, movies, user-generated content, and news. One of the most important things that intelligent people do is make recommendations. Recommender systems predict your needs and preferences from past interactions with you, your explicit preferences, and learned preferences using methods called collaborative and content filtering. Trillions of item descriptions are stored ready to be recommended to billions of people.[35]

Governments are using AI to fight wars that seemed impossible only twenty years ago. Future increased and enhanced developments of the capabilities described in the following articles will increase the confidence Satan and his followers have that they can win a war against God and Jesus in the Battle of Armageddon at the end of the Tribulation. These articles also depict how easy it could be to destroy humanity through AI.

The following article appeared in The Jerusalem Post and it describes how Israel in the conflict with Hamas in Gaza in the spring of 2021 used successfully the developments in technology and artificial intelligence in war.

Current and future advancements enable the militaries of the world to conduct war in a new fashion.

The Israeli military is calling Operation Guardian of the Walls the first artificial-intelligence war.

"For the first time, artificial intelligence was a key component and power multiplier in fighting the enemy," an IDF Intelligence Corps senior officer said. "This is a first-of-its-kind campaign for the IDF. We implemented new methods of operation and used technological developments that were a force multiplier for the entire IDF."

IDF Unit 9900's satellites have gathered intelligence information over the years. They were able to automatically detect changes in terrain in real time so that during the operation, the military was able to detect launching positions and hit them after firing.

For example, Unit 9900 troops using satellite imagery were able to detect 14 rocket launchers that were located next to a school.

To destroy underground tunnels, "Years of work, out-of-the-box thinking, and the fusion of all the power of the intelligence division together with elements in the field led to the breakthrough solution of the underground," the senior officer said. Using the data gathered and analyzed through AI, the Israeli Air Force was able to use the appropriate munitions to hit a target, whether an apartment, a tunnel, or a building.[36]

Military advancements in AI are top-secret. Can you imagine how advanced they have become?

The artificial intelligence industry in China is a rapidly developing multi-billion-dollar industry. Since 2006, China has steadily developed a national agenda for artificial intelligence development, and has emerged as one of the leading nations in artificial intelligence research and development

The State Council of China issued *"A Next Generation Artificial Intelligence Development Plan"* on July 8, 2017, in which the Central Committee and the State Council urged the governing bodies of China to promote the development of artificial intelligence. Specifically, the plan describes AI as a "strategic technology" that has become a "focus of international competition. The document urges significant investment in several strategic areas related to AI and calls for close cooperation between the state and private sector.

Chinese authorities now have six years of experience building up their AI regulatory knowhow since they launched their Next Generation Artificial Intelligence Development Plan. They're using regulation as a form of industrial policy, in addition to traditional subsidies. "If China can be first on AI governance, it can project those standards and regulations globally, shaping lucrative financial markets."[37]

China's management of its AI program contrasts with that of the United States. In general, few boundaries exist between Chinese commercial companies, university research laboratories, the military, and the central government. As a result, the Chinese government has a direct means of guiding AI development priorities and accessing technology that was ostensibly developed for civilian purposes. To further strengthen these ties, the Chinese government created in January 2017 a Military-Civil Fusion Development Commission, which is intended to speed the transfer of AI technology from commercial companies and research institutions to the military.

The following article in the Washington Post makes me feel uncomfortable about how AI could be used before the Rapture.

By Gerrit De Vynck

July 7, 2021

The U.S. says humans will always be in control of AI weapons. But the age of autonomous war is already here.

The Pentagon says a ban on AI weapons is not necessary. But missiles, guns and drones that think for themselves are already killing people in combat and have been for years.

Picture a desert battlefield, scarred by years of warfare. A retreating army scrambles to escape as its enemy advances. Dozens of small drones, indistinguishable from the quadcopters used by hobbyists and filmmakers, come buzzing down from the sky, using cameras to scan the terrain and onboard computers to decide on their own what looks like a target. Suddenly they begin dive bombing trucks and individual soldiers, exploding on contact and causing even more panic and confusion.

This is not a science fiction imagining of what future wars might be like. It is a real scene that played out last spring as soldiers loyal to the Libyan strongman Khalifa Hifter retreated from the Turkish-backed forces of the Libyan government. According to a U.N. group of weapons and legal experts appointed to document the conflict, drones that can operate without human control "hunted down" Hifter's soldiers as they fled.

Today, efforts to enact a total ban on lethal autonomous weapons, long demanded by human rights activists, are now being supported by 30 countries. But the world's leading military powers insist that isn't necessary. The U.S. military says concerns are overblown, and humans can effectively control autonomous weapons, while Russia's government says true AI weapons can't be banned because they don't exist yet.

But the facts on the ground show that technological advancements, coupled with complex conflicts like the Syrian and Libyan civil wars, have created a reality where weapons that make their own decisions are already killing people.[38]

ChatGPT

Let's take a deeper look at one of the latest technological wonders that was briefly described earlier and how it could benefit us.

ChatGPT is an artificial intelligence model that is able to generate text in a conversational way. It adopts a dialogue format that makes it possible to chat with the tool in a natural language. ChatGPT can answer follow-up questions, admit its mistakes, reject certain requests that it deems inappropriate or unethical, and solve many complex problems.

The capabilities of ChatGPT are hard to even imagine — from coding, translating, and proofreading text to using ChatGPT for influencer marketing. Here are the results of a survey of internet users:

- An astounding 70% of respondents believe that ChatGPT will eventually take over Google as a primary search engine. This means that the internet as we know it might soon be over.
- Almost 40% of people are afraid that ChatGPT will destroy the job market.
- As many as 60% respondents would allow ChatGPT to offer medical advice and give health-related consultations.
- Only 9% of the respondents would not use ChatGPT for academic purposes, while more than 57% would let ChatGPT write their thesis for them.
- More than 86% believe that ChatGPT could be used to manipulate and control the population.[39]

These articles are scary enough, but realize AI is still in its infant stage. Advancements are occurring at such a rapid rate that one and two-year-old AI applications are probably outdated and obsolete. Can you imagine what new capabilities will exist in three more years?

What is driving all these advancements?

Money and the drive for more profits!

A popular verse often quote about money is:

> "[10]...the love of money is a root of all kinds of evil." (1 Timothy 6:10)

Big Tech is using money from big businesses to develop and create a world controlled by computer systems. When a new enhanced system is delivered, typical responses from users are, "wow look what we have done and how much better it is than the old system. How did we live without this capability?" Typically, what happens next is the users will conjure up new ideas to further improve the system. For some this becomes an endless pursuit of "perfection," to maximize efficiency and increase profits.

These developments can be compared to the time when the Tower of Babel was being built. For governments, technology is now an essential element for their defense, or aggression against their foes. They can give the military a false sense of invincibility. In the medical and scientific fields, some professionals even begin thinking they are like God. These radical new technological advances can result in sins of pride, arrogance, and self-exaltation. God will permit Big Tech to continue delivering amazing new capabilities up to the Tribulation when the plagues and natural disasters will disrupt the development and use of these new technologies.

As noted in a previous chapter, the term Big Tech is commonly used to mean Facebook (META), Twitter, Google, and Amazon. In this book, Big Tech refers to META, Twitter (X), Google, Apple, Amazon, and Microsoft (the Big Six).

Each of these companies collect your personal data in many different ways – most of the time without your knowledge of what they do with it. Sometimes they do it illegally. They each have fought off numerous lawsuits for invasion of personal privacy. They have been found guilty multiple times by governments around the world and their fines are staggering.

The European Union (EU) fined Google $5 billion in 2018. France fined Google $592 million in 2021 and Amazon $888 million in 2021. The U.S. Federal Trade Commission fined Facebook $5 billion in 2020. The European Data Protection Board fined Instagram, which is owned by Meta Platforms, roughly $400 million for allegedly violating European data privacy laws regarding the handling of children's data. The EU fined META $1.3 billion in 2023. Microsoft also has had major legal conflicts with the EU with fines of $2.4 billion. Despite all these fines and legal costs, they continue to profit greatly while violating individual privacy and reselling our data.

The Number of Social Media Users Around the World

As of 2022, the United States has the third-largest social media audience worldwide, after China and India. It is home to over 302 million social media users at a social networking penetration rate of 90 percent.[40]

China has the world's largest number of people at 1.4 billion and in January 2023 had 1.03 billion active social media users which equates to 72% of its total population.[41] China has developed capabilities and intricate databases to monitor their citizens. Baidu,

Alibaba, and Tencent are China's three largest technology titans. Baidu is their equivalent to Google. The Alibaba Group offers a variety of e-commerce services with the domestic retail segment being its largest revenue generator which rivals Amazon. The WeChat and QQ apps are social media messaging apps.

For comparison, Russia only has 106 million social media users which equates to 73% of their population. A total of 227.0 million cellular mobile connections were active in Russia in early 2023, with this figure equivalent to 156.9 percent of the total population.[42] Russia is the home for major cybercriminal rings, hackers, and cyberwarfare/espionage. These skills may be valuable to the Antichrist in the establishment and enforcement of his one-world government.

Europe has a population of 742 million.[43] In 2019, before the coronavirus pandemic, the number of e-commerce stood at around 451 million, which has now risen to approximately 540 million in 2023.[44]

These comparisons are being made because China and America are probably among the first nations where the Antichrist will take control of their computer systems, because of their high levels of online users and because their systems are generally the most advanced.

We can't really say how China controls its internet companies because the data available cannot be verified. Considering the authoritarian rule generally exercised by the Chinese Communist Party (which seems to be growing even stricter), it is likely these companies are in the government's grip and that grip is tightening.

The size and scope of the six Big Tech companies is demonstrated by their estimated numbers of users and their relative ranking in the Fortune 500 companies:

The Roles of Big Tech, Big Media, and Big Government

6/5/2023	Fortune 500 Rank	# Users Worldwide
Google (Alphabet)	8	4.3 Billion
Facebook (Meta)	31	3 Billion
Twitter (X)	597	540 Million
Amazon	2	310 Million
Apple	4	588 Million
Microsoft	13	145 Million

Each of these companies occupy a major space in Big Media so there is overlap among their users (many people likely are users of all six companies).

Big Media Wants Your Personal Information From Big Tech

Here is a succinct summarized article describing how Big Tech became "Big." It also dramatically describes why they want your personal information.

> Big Tech companies have a tremendous impact on our lives. Nearly every citizen uses their services. These companies have expanded at a breathtaking speed and have created more and more services, and here lies the problem.
>
> META owns and manages among others: Facebook, Instagram, and WhatsApp. Mark Zuckerberg (META CEO) knew exactly what he was doing when he acquired Instagram and WhatsApp. His company bought its two main competitors, and in a way, killed the competition.
>
> Google has created services such as Gmail, Google AdWords, AdSense, Google analytics, and the list goes on and on.
>
> Amazon has become the marketplace of everything, from pins to sophisticated devices to anything you can type in the search bar. In 2017 Amazon acquired Whole Foods. By June 2018, Amazon had fully integrated Whole Foods stores into its Prime membership program enabling groceries to be purchased online.

To survive, many small retailers have been forced to sell their products through Amazon Marketplace. An unexpected problem for Amazon is the number of counterfeit items being sold ranging from cosmetics, clothing, shoes, and toys. Most of these products come from China. A new report from Amazon reveals it blocked 10 billion attempted counterfeit listings in 2020 - up from 6 billion from the year before—and destroyed 2 million fake goods in its warehouses.[45]

Whether businesses are start-ups, medium-sized businesses, or even large enterprises, nobody is safe from the competition of the major Big Tech companies. How are their competitors removed from the market? They either manipulate the market by lowering prices up to 50% or by flat out offering services for "free." Or, they can acquire their competitors.

These companies' primary interest is data! Billions of users' data. The Big Tech companies take the data of their users and sell it to advertisers, or use it to understand their users better.

Additionally, these colossal companies like to capture as much market share as possible. Traditional big box stores like Home Depot, Lowes, Target, Walmart, Best Buy, and thousands of others have established online sites to expand their market share.

Nearly 90% of computers globally use Microsoft Windows. The number is staggering – 1.5 billion Windows users (includes 200 million older versions of Windows).[46] Now Microsoft also sells its Surface laptops and creates software for a lot of services like MS Office and MS Mail. Big Tech companies have made it their goal to penetrate every market niche and to drive competition out.

All the Big Tech companies spy on you. Google and META are the most obvious even though they try to hide it with continuous "transparency policies." Microsoft tracks every move you do on your desktop. They call this telemetry, and Cortana, their AI assistant, monitors everything you say through the microphone. If the option is on, and of course in most cases it is on by default, it must be manually turned off.

Amazon gathers everything you do on their site, from purchasing patterns, to clicks, to just simple views on a product. Then they bombard your browser with stuff you could potentially buy. At first glance, it all seems nice because they will understand you better and they will be able to offer a better experience. However, isn't it spooky that the moment you talk about fitness, you get sponsored ads about a protein shake? Or better yet, gym-related products like dumbbells?[47]

How will a national database be developed in the U.S. to surveil its citizens? One driver will be pressure from the CDC to develop a database of citizens taking the COVID-19 vaccination.

Millions of adults vaccinated against COVID-19 have little to prove it beyond a paper card they received at inoculation sites. The U.S. has no central database for immunizations. Most states have limited records of immunizations. As restrictions for employment, entry into business establishments, major events or travel to countries that require proof of vaccinations, the demand for a national database is increasing.

The following was taken from the U.S.'s CDC website in August 2021 describing their evolving database. It is only a matter of time before it is expanded to either have direct links to state databases with the names of vaccinated people, or the state databases will be merged into a national database registry.

COVID-19 Vaccine Data Systems

Tracking COVID-19 vaccine distribution and administration activities requires collaboration between public and private information technology (IT) systems and integration of existing and newly developed IT systems.

A strong, nationally coordinated approach is critical to collect, track, and analyze vaccination data, especially in the early phases of vaccine administration.[48]

The World Health Organization (WHO) published a 99-page document on its website giving guidelines for establishing a database which can be used for many things such as proof of vaccination. This data could be used to restrict international travel.

Digital documentation of COVID-19 certificates: vaccination status: technical specifications and implementation guidance, 27 August 2021.

This is a guidance document for countries and implementing partners on the technical requirements for developing digital information systems for issuing standards-based interoperable digital certificates for COVID-19 vaccination status, and considerations for implementation of such systems, for the purposes of continuity of care, and proof of vaccination.[49]

Increasing pressure to verify vaccinated people will probably result in the near future the development of one massive database of vaccinated and unvaccinated people is highly probable. How will it be used raises many concerns since it can be used in multiple ways to infringe not only on our privacy.

As IT development and applications mature, look for an off-the-shelf database to be available with the flexibility to solve the aging computer systems our government uses today. If the government was a commercial company, the current inefficiencies and service costs would have spelled their doom thirty years ago and they would be out-of-business. A massive overhaul of the outdated federal computing systems using systems and technology from Big Tech will happen faster if more social programs are approved by Congress.

Like every other program, the scope will increase over time so it will ultimately contain all your personal information, e.g., social security information, health history (so people who supposedly have mental illness can be identified to prevent them from purchasing firearms), criminal history, and personal financial records for the IRS.

Now let's examine Big Media and their influence.

Here is a good quote to ponder when you are trying to figure out what to believe from Big Media.

"The people will believe what the media tells them they believe." - George Orwell.

How much of the news do you believe?

Chapter 7

Big Media

Previously, Big Tech was compared to a thunderstorm which is the beginning of a hurricane. As the thunderstorm develops into a tropical depression, it needs a continuous supply of energy from warm ocean water and warm moist air before it grows into a hurricane. The Perfect Political Storm is building to strike our nation and Big Media is delivering unprecedented (and still-growing) amounts of "hot air" to fuel the demise of the United States through its continuously-biased reporting about many contentious subjects.

Distortion and bias take many forms. Sometimes Big Media misrepresents the facts or fabricates news out of fiction. Other times, important information is ignored or hidden because it is inconsistent with the story that Big Media is trying to sell to you. Please remember, there is an overlap between Big Tech social media and Big Media's traditional media types.

The following quote should be the ultimate benchmark for a non-biased media.

> "We all have our likes and our dislikes. But... when we are doing news - when we are doing the front-page news, not the back page, not the op-ed pages, but when we are doing the daily news, covering politics - it is our duty to be sure that we do not permit our prejudices to show. That is simply basic journalism."
> Walter Cronkite

Here are two quotes that reflect the content the American people presently receive daily.

> "The lowest form of popular culture - lack of information, misinformation, disinformation, and a contempt for the truth or the reality of most people's lives - has overrun real journalism. Today,

ordinary Americans are being stuffed with garbage." Carl Bernstein

"Fake news is a big thing in the field of Social Media Journalism. Fake news can be as simple as spreading mis-information, or as dangerous as smearing hateful propaganda." Fabrizio Moreira

The media are important to the functioning of the United States government. Democracy cannot function without communication. For voters to make informed choices among candidates, the voters must learn about the candidates' policy positions, track records, personalities, and experience. This happens with the exchange of information from candidates to voters. Traditionally, newspapers, radio and TV performed this function. But now these traditional news channels are highly dependent upon Big Tech, which redistributes their news reporting online. Big Media acts as gatekeepers, deciding which news stories and information will be emphasized, which will be buried deeply, and which are blocked completely.

Today, this communication can happen directly through Big Tech's social media platforms. A candidate sends messages directly to voters skipping the traditional news channel "middlemen." Former President Trump used Twitter successfully to tweet a list of followers that grew from a couple million to 89 million after he was elected President before his Twitter account was permanently suspended.

To continue the analysis of the rapid increase in technology and knowledge predicted in the book of Daniel, here is a brief overview of the historical role of the media in America and how it has helped spread knowledge. In some ways, not much has changed in the degree of venom and bitter criticism, but the speed and number of mediums to deliver the news have dramatically increased.

Newspapers have been intertwined with and integral to democracy since the founding of the U.S. The Federalist Papers were first published in newspapers in New York in 1787-88 to promote the ratification of the United States Constitution.

In the first years of the American republic, leaflets, posters, and local newspapers provided both news and opinion, often tightly interwoven.

The 1800 presidential election (Thomas Jefferson versus John Adams) is still remembered for its vicious "attack ads."

For much of American history until the early twentieth century, most newspapers were simply the voices of the political parties. This type of journalism is called partisan journalism. Other newspapers practiced yellow journalism, reporting shocking and sordid stories to attract readers and sell more papers. Objective reporting, also called descriptive reporting, did not appear until the early twentieth century.

Media Influence

The news media has influenced public opinion and politics throughout American history. A prominent - and notorious - early example is the role of William Randolph Hearst's newspapers in starting the Spanish-American War in 1898. Hearst's papers ran many stories chronicling the cruelty of Spanish colonial rule. When the American battleship Maine exploded in Spanish-ruled Havana harbor under mysterious circumstances, Hearst seized the moment, alleging that the Spanish had destroyed the ship (the cause is still the subject of debate). War soon followed. Hyperbolic fake news is nothing new!

Today, few media moguls have the direct influence of William Randolph Hearst, but the combined effect of media consolidation plus Big Tech has renewed the concern that the media has too much power. Television and the internet make good use of yellow journalism by running sensationalized news stories that are all too often less-than-well-researched. But the best example of yellow journalism can be found today in social media venues such as Twitter or Facebook.

Newspapers

Newspapers are a critical part of the American news landscape, but they have been hit hard as more and more Americans consume news digitally. Circulation numbers for daily weekday newspapers peaked in 1987 at 63 million (no digital subscriptions existed). The estimated total U.S. daily newspaper circulation of print only was 2.6 million in 2023.[50] Printed news magazines have followed a similar path of decline.

Radio / Television

Election Day, November 2, 1920, marked the beginning of news radio as we know it today. The radio station KDKA in Pittsburgh, Pennsylvania became the first licensed commercial radio station to produce a news program. The launch was timed to allow listeners to learn the results of the election closer to real time without having to wait to read about it in the newspaper.

Today was the first morning news program to be broadcast on American television and in the world, when it debuted on January 14, 1952. The earliest national evening news program was The Walter Compton News, a short-lived 15-minute newscast that aired on the DuMont Television Network from 1947 to 1948.[51]

Though there are many television and radio broadcast stations operating in America, most are heavily dependent on syndicated news provided by a few providers (usually the Big Media television and cable networks). The way news is presented and selected is largely determined by cable news networks.

Smartphones / Cable News / Social Media

The smartphone age and the 24-hour cable news-cycle have reshaped what Americans expect from their news outlets. The transition of news from print, television and radio to digital spaces has caused huge disruptions in the traditional news industry, especially the print news industry. More than eight-in-ten U.S. adults say they get news from a smartphone, computer, or tablet "often" or "sometimes," including 60% who say they do so often.[52]

In the 21st century, there has been a consolidation of the news media due to business closures and mergers. About 15 billionaires and six corporations own most of the U.S. media outlets. The biggest media conglomerates in America are AT&T, Comcast, The Walt Disney Company, National Amusements (which includes Viacom Inc. and CBS), News Corp and Fox Corporation (which are both owned in part by the Murdoch family), Sony, and Hearst Communications. Comcast owns NBC and MSNBC, Walt Disney owns ABC and ESPN, AT&T owns CNN, and National Amusements owns CBS.[53] Many of these companies own newspapers, radio and television stations, and web news sites. Several are also in motion picture production. The Wall Street Journal and Fox News have ownership in common.

Mergers and acquisitions typically result in cost-cutting and consolidation, and media reporting and research staffs have dwindled. Much of their content now comes from reprints from other news media, e.g., usually the Washington Post and New York Times, news services like the Associated Press, press releases, and unverified leaks from progressive politicians and activists. Most of Big Media has left-leaning editorial boards and executives, which influence their news reporting and editorial positions.

Because of the potential threat of losing their jobs in a shrinking labor market, today's journalists and broadcast analysts report the news in line with the agenda of their bosses. Most journalists today have insufficient budgets and time to devote to research and validate new stories.

In addition, most of these companies are members of the Associated Press, which freely shares common news stories with members. Therefore, if one journalist publishes an article that is non-factual, it can be spread across the nation quickly. However, if a retraction is made, the retraction is seldom printed in the other outlets that carried the original story. The public suffers greatly with this news sharing arrangement.

To keep costs low, Big Media often hires young inexperienced writers, many of whom are educated and indoctrinated by left-leaning professors. For reasons of speed, sloth, or dogma, they do not fact-check or seek multiple sources for articles they write. This is especially true when the subject is in line with the current progressive narrative. This arrangement of "quoting" or "reposting" a news article can have extremely negative effects if the story is not factual. Network and cable news outlets follow the same pattern, but they also put a premium on appearance. Their on-air personalities must look good and exhibit charisma on camera while reading from a teleprompter.

The media have given political parties the tools to reach large numbers of people. If it chooses, it can inform them without bias on key issues ranging from policies, election platforms, and can investigate and report incompetent, negligent or dishonest acts of officials. In theory, the media should be an enabler for democracy, leading to better-educated voters and a more legitimate government. The media should be an independent force that helps the public hold elected officials accountable for their misdeeds.

Unfortunately, the media no longer is performing this role. Today, the focus in the news media has shifted to an agenda set forth by the corporate officers, sometimes at the behest of their owners. Their primary goals are (1) to increase market share to drive up profits, and (2) to advance their own social and political goals. Even though this sometimes leads to losses in viewers and subscribers, which leads to less market share and profit, they often give the greatest emphasis to their social and political agenda. CNN is an example of a liberal network that has lost millions of viewers because of their biased reporting.

Major networks like ABC, CBS, NBC, CNN, and Fox News carefully select the primary anchors not only on their ability to be personable and clearly articulating the news, but ascertain that their political and social views align with their companies. Leading newspapers place a similar emphasis on political and social views for their news and editorial staff.

For example, CNN and MSNBC play to a liberal base and would never put a die-hard vocal Trump supporter in a prime-time anchor slot. Conversely, one of CNN's liberal anchors would never be hired by Fox News.

Another trend in broadcast media is the hiring of ex-politicians, military commanders, and doctors to add commentaries to their telecasts. These folks are paid to add an "expert" opinion to validate the corporation's agenda. Those who are favorable toward Big Government views typically are hired by left-leaning networks, those who are more conservative are hired by Fox News.

Fox News, the Wall Street Journal, the Washington Times, and the New York Post newspapers and many radio talk-shows and podcasts have moderate or conservative-leaning political and social views.

Virtually all the other major news media (broadcast, cable, newspapers, magazines, and news agencies) lean to the left.

Cable news companies even have internet homepages to enable a news-starved nation to view the latest news immediately. Cable news, cell phones, and the internet bombard us with news 24 hours per day 7 days per week. Continuously. Non-stop. Never-ending. Millions of people have become news "addicts or news junkies."

Social Media

When electronic communication via email was introduced in 1965, the speed of communication went from "snail mail" taking days or weeks to only seconds. Everyone marveled at this new tool. The inception of Facebook in 2004 changed the world and how it communicates. Communication using email is personal – you choose the audience to communicate with.

META is a social networking site that makes it easy for you to connect and share with family and friends online by sending messages and posting status updates to keep in touch. You can also share different types of content, like photos and links. But unlike email or instant messaging, which are relatively private, the things you share on META are more public, which means they will usually be seen by many other people unless you choose to restrict your content.

In March 2018, an anonymous whistleblower (later revealed to be former Cambridge Analytica employee Christopher Wylie) revealed to the press that during the 2016 election, Cambridge Analytica used a misleading app to collect personal information on users and their friends' META profiles without their consent.

The information collected was subsequently used to build data profiles on users, which were then used for targeted political advertising. Although only 270,000 people downloaded the app, it is estimated that over 50 million META users were affected, due to the large number of likes and reposts that some ads received. This social media strategy was used in the 2016 presidential campaigns of Donald Trump.

META CEO Mark Zuckerberg and whistleblower Christopher Wylie were called to testify before Congress. Cambridge Analytica was liquidated for generating the data and Facebook META was fined $5 billion. This scandal created a global debate about the ethics surrounding data harvesting and privacy, especially in political contexts, but also how consumer purchasing data was being gathered.

Twitter came into existence in 2006. Twitter is a "microblogging" system that allows you to send and receive short posts called tweets. Tweets can be up to 140 characters long and can include links to relevant websites and resources. Twitter users follow other users. If you follow someone you can see their tweets in your twitter 'timeline'.

Elon Musk's $44 billion acquisition of Twitter was finalized in October 2022 and the company is now privately owned. Musk initiated a series of reforms and management changes. Musk went to work and immediately:

- reinstated a number of previously banned accounts.
- reduced the workforce by approximately 80%.
- closed one of Twitter's three data centers.
- largely eliminated the content moderation team and replaced it with a new feature called Community Notes.
- instituted a plan that charged personal users $8 per month to get a *verified* blue badge and $1,000 per month for an organizational gold badge.[54]

One of the newer apps is TikTok. TikTok is a social media platform for creating, sharing, and discovering short videos. The app is used by young people as an outlet to express themselves through singing, dancing, comedy, and lip-syncing by allowing users to create videos and share them across a community.

The app was originally Musical.ly until August 2018, when the app was taken over by a Chinese company ByteDance and its users were moved to TikTok. The U.S. government tried to ban the app, contending TikTok data on American citizens could be sent back to authorities in Beijing. A federal judge ruled against the ban in

September 2020 and use of the app continues. However, as of April 2023, at least 34 (of 50) states have announced or enacted bans on state government agencies, employees, and contractors using TikTok on government-issued devices. State bans only affect government employees and do not prohibit civilians from having or using the app on their personal devices.[55]

The power of social media to influence our lives is amazing. Many people believe The Antichrist will use apps like TikTok for faking miracles to promote his desire for a one- world religion.

The top two websites in the world are Google and YouTube (which Google owns). Google is the most-used search engine in the world. An estimated 122 million people view YouTube daily. In 2020, the third most-visited website was META. Instagram is a text-free platform that is visual with audio. META owns Instagram. Unlike META, which provides text, audio and video/picture services, or Twitter, which relies on text alone, Instagram's sole purpose is to enable users to share images or videos with their audience.

More than 23 billion cell phone text messages (SMS – Short Messaging Service) are sent every day. An estimated 6 billion people worldwide are projected to own cell phones by 2025, or 78% of the population of the world.[56]

When the Rapture occurs, there will be so much confusion, the Antichrist must be able to communicate quickly with the world. Initially, all existing communication media will remain intact. There is currently no faster way for the Antichrist to communicate and control communication than using social media and text messaging.

As the Antichrist assumes more power, communication mediums will be utilized to inform the people of the world of his coming plans for the new one-world order. The Antichrist will take control of the major communications industries, reduce the number of different companies down to a minimum, and may nationalize them under a central government.

As the End Times judgments progress and increase in severity, traditional land-based cell towers, television, and radio towers, and underground cable systems will be destroyed. To maintain control, the Antichrist will use the government's and Big Tech's satellites to fill this void. The next generation of cell phones will become as capable as today's satellite phones and their price will drop dramatically once mass production begins. Some of the early versions of these new satellite cell phones are being distributed today.

Social media's role in the End Times is a critical asset to the Antichrist to influence the people in all nations to embrace his one-world government.

How does a Christian navigate through the current conundrum of news to determine the truth?

> *"*[15]*See then that you walk circumspectly, not as fools but as wise,* [16]*redeeming the time, because the days are evil." (Ephesians 5:15-16)*

Unfortunately, my contention is there is no way to easily ascertain whether what you see, hear, or read is the truth. The number of instances in the last two or three years where all types of media misreported on politicians, celebrities, sports figures, and wealthy individuals by presenting intentional mis-information, fake news, and out-and-out lies could fill an entire large book.

The following illustration may help understand how the media operates and misbehaves.

Have you ever heard of the Fourth Estate and Fifth Column?

Possibly not, so let me provide you with the best description available because it applies to today's media outlets and personalities.

The fourth estate refers to journalists and the business of journalism. Here is the classic explanation of the first three estates:

> "In May 1789, King Louis XVI of France summoned to Versailles a full meeting of the 'Estate's Generals. The First Estate consisted of three hundred clergy. The Second Estate, three hundred nobles. The Third Estate, six hundred commoners. Some years later, after the French Revolution, Edmund Burke, looking up at the Press Gallery of the House of Commons, said,

'Yonder sits the Fourth Estate, and they are more important than them all."

There was no fifth estate so how did a fifth column get added?

The fifth column refers to revolutionaries, rabble-rousers that work secretly or in a clandestine fashion within an organization or country.

Here is the probable explanation of the fifth column.

In a 1936 radio address by Emilio Mola, an insurgent general during the 1936-39 Spanish Civil War addressed the nation as his army approached Madrid. He broadcast a message that the four columns of his forces outside the city would be supported by a "fifth column" of his supporters inside the city, intent on undermining the *(Spanish)* Republican government from within.[57]

For illustration purposes, the fifth column in this book is the liberal media. In its drive to become big and highly profitable, Big Media does not have a healthy fourth column (press and media) producing well-thought-out editorials and investigative reporting which is critical to the functioning of a healthy democracy. True journalists are a dying breed and are finding it increasingly difficult to stay employed.

An additional part of this new fifth column is the *swamp* in Washington, D.C. The swamp is composed of lobbyists, bureaucrats and professional politicians who are more interested in lining their own pockets while accumulating more power and prestige than looking out for the welfare of their constituents and the best interests of our nation. These politicians and lobbyists (many are ex-Congressmen), "leak" insider information which often is government classified or secret to the rogue journalists to push their own agendas, or to embarrass and discredit their opponents.

My belief is that these liberal rogue journalists and the swamp have become the fifth column, intent on spreading their beliefs in socialism while supporting the left's political candidates and agendas. They hate a "free" America and want to destroy it.

The Roles of Big Tech, Big Media, and Big Government

There are often commercial and political incentives for independent media to provide news and information that caters to their political beliefs and ideologies. This increases intolerance and creates an opportunity for leaders of opposition groups to mobilize. We are seeing this today through the efforts of Black Lives Matter, Critical Race Theory, Antifa, LBGTQ, and the promotion of WOKE culture and philosophy.

Big Media and the fifth column have become one of the greatest threats to the government of the United States in a long time, and too few people are conscious of the danger.

To bring this matter of media overreach into our lives, here is the latest development that overlaps both Big Media and Big Government.

Major issues American citizens face are coming to the surface that serve as warnings our freedoms and especially freedom of speech is at risk.

Control of Free Speech

The Disinformation Governance Board (DGB) was an advisory board of the United States Department of Homeland Security (DHS), announced on April 27, 2022. The board's stated function was to protect national security by disseminating guidance to DHS agencies on combating misinformation that threatens the security of the homeland. Specific problem areas mentioned by the DHS include false information propagated by human smugglers encouraging migrants to surge to the Mexico–United States border, as well as Russian-state disinformation on election interference and the 2022 Russian invasion of Ukraine.[58] The following summary describes what happened and what is ongoing between Big Media and Big Government.

> The Department of Homeland Security is quietly broadening its efforts to curb speech it considers dangerous. Years of internal DHS memos, emails, and documents — obtained via leaks and an ongoing lawsuit, as well as public documents — illustrate an expansive effort by the agency to influence media platforms.

When DHS announced a new "Disinformation Governance Board in April 2023, it was widely ridiculed, immediately scaled back, and then shut down within a few months. However, other initiatives are underway as DHS pivots to monitoring social media now that its original mandate — the war on terror — has been wound down.

Behind closed doors, and through pressure on private platforms, the U.S. government has used its power to try to shape online discourse. According to meeting minutes and other records appended to a lawsuit filed by Missouri Attorney General Eric Schmitt reveal that DHS discussions have ranged from the scale and scope of government intervention in online discourse to the mechanics of streamlining takedown requests for false or intentionally misleading information on social media platforms.

A strategic document reveals the underlying work is ongoing.

- DHS plans to target inaccurate information on "the origins of the COVID-19 pandemic and the efficacy of COVID-19 vaccines, racial justice, U.S. withdrawal from Afghanistan, and the nature of U.S. support to Ukraine."
- META created a special portal for DHS and government partners to report disinformation directly.

There is also a formalized process for government officials to directly flag content on META or Instagram and request that it be throttled or suppressed through a special META portal that requires a government or law enforcement email to use.

How disinformation is defined by the government has not been clearly articulated, and the inherently subjective nature of what constitutes disinformation provides a broad opening for DHS officials to make politically motivated determinations about what constitutes dangerous speech.

DHS justifies these goals — which have expanded far beyond its original purview on foreign threats to encompass disinformation originating domestically — by claiming that terrorist threats can be "exacerbated by misinformation and disinformation spread online."

The Roles of Big Tech, Big Media, and Big Government

But the laudable goal of protecting Americans from danger has often been used to conceal political maneuvering.

The extent to which the DHS initiatives affect Americans' daily social feeds is unclear. During the 2020 election, the government flagged numerous posts as suspicious, many of which were then taken down, documents cited in the Missouri attorney general's lawsuit disclosed.

Prior to the 2020 election, tech companies including Twitter, META, Reddit, Discord, Wikipedia, Microsoft, LinkedIn, and Verizon Media met on a monthly basis with the FBI, CISA, and other government representatives. According to NBC News, the meetings were part of an initiative, still ongoing, between the private sector and government to discuss how firms would handle misinformation during the election.[59]

The following summarizes what a Federal Court judge has ruled.

President Biden's social media manipulation is exactly what the Framers feared. By Jeffrey M. McCall, July 07, 2023.

The nation's constitutional framers worked hard to create a government that responded to its citizens' interests rather than telling citizens what their interests should be. The framers feared a government that could control the flow of information and impose its views on the governed. The First Amendment was created to allow for citizens, not the government, to manage the marketplace of ideas.

Federal District Judge Terry Doughty clearly understands this principle, as evidenced by the preliminary injunction he handed out recently that restricts the Biden administration from manipulating and pressuring social media outlets for its own messaging purposes. It's a safe bet that every single signer of the original Constitution would have agreed with Judge Doughty. Such was their fear of and opposition to government control of the rhetorical sphere.

The order expressed appropriate concern that "the present case arguably involves the most massive attack against free speech in

United States' history." The temporary order prohibits the government from contacting social media companies for the purpose of managing "the removal, deletion, suppression, or reduction of content containing protected free speech posted on social-media platforms."

Judge Doughty believes the government "used its power to silence the opposition" on a wide range of topics, from COVID practices to Biden administration policies to Hunter Biden's laptop controversy. In essence, the government's attempt to stifle alleged misinformation ignored the rights of American citizens to engage in free debate, which includes being able to say non-government-approved things, some of which might be outlandish.

Of course, opponents of Judge Doughty's ruling were quick to point out that he was appointed by former President Trump, as though that fact disqualifies Doughty from being capable of sniffing out constitutional free speech infringements. The shrill voices against Doughty also waved the bloody shirt of misinformation, worrying that Americans are too stupid to reason for themselves and thus must be manipulated by big government, browbeating compliant social media outlets to do its bidding along the way.

The First Amendment protects rumors, conspiracy theories, half-truths and even falsehoods. That's because, as constitutional framer James Madison well knew, sometimes the government-approved points of view turn out to be misguided, and the so-called falsehoods have nuggets of truth in them. Further, there are ways to address potential misinformation with counter-messaging, rather than by stifling voices.[60]

The FBI and School Board Investigations

In September 2021, following threats voiced against school officials for promoting Critical Race Theory, transgender policies, and pornographic books, the National School Boards Association wrote a letter to President Joe Biden requesting assistance to address concerns about school employees' and board members' safety.

The Roles of Big Tech, Big Media, and Big Government

On Oct. 4, 2021, Attorney General Merrick Garland sent a five-paragraph memo to the FBI and federal prosecutors acknowledging a "disturbing spike in harassment, intimidation, and threats of violence" against school officials. Garland directed the FBI to hold meetings across the country and bring together government leaders to discuss strategies to address those threats.

Information from a whistleblower revealed the FBI was compiling threat assessments related to parents and created a "threat tag" called EDUOFFICIALS. "The FBI uses "threat tags" to track information and spot trends — it does not necessarily signal a full investigation, which occurs if there is evidence of potential violence and violation of federal law, an FBI official stated. House Republicans on the Judiciary Committee published a report in November that said the FBI had opened investigations with the EDUOFFICIALS threat tag in almost every region of the country, according to a whistleblower.

This memo led claim that parents who "challenge school curriculums" were being labeled "domestic terrorists."[61]

Investigation of Catholics

House Judiciary Committee Chairman Jim Jordan sent a letter to FBI Director Christopher Wray revealing that the FBI Richmond Field Office coordinated in February 2023 with multiple FBI field offices across the country to produce the memo targeting traditional Catholics as potential domestic terrorists.

A leaked memo from the FBI's Richmond, Virginia, field office, published on the internet in February of this year, discussed investigating "radical traditionalist" Catholics who the bureau alleged may have been part of a "far-right white nationalist movement."[62] This investigation is ongoing and has raised a lot of eyebrows.

Do you find these reports alarming?

Here is another quote about Big Media to close this chapter, and it seems to apply to Big Government as well.

> "I operate under the assumption that the mass media will never be accurate. ... It operates with the objective to simplify and

exaggerate, which is exactly what Walt Disney told his cartoonists." Michael Crichton – American author who has sold over 200 million books worldwide.

Chapter 8

Big Government

The Big Tech thunderstorm has emerged as a small hurricane over the Atlantic Ocean and the hot air from Big Media is increasing its intensity. The final element required for the "Perfect Political Storm" is for the prevailing winds to carry it to the United States as a Category 5 hurricane to enable Big Government to get bigger and bigger.

Politicians in the local, city, state, and federal governments are supersensitive to the prevailing winds better known as public sentiment which is typically embellished by the liberal media. All politicians are keenly aware of the principle in nature: "only the fittest survive." Politicians are like chameleons. In our pop culture, a chameleon is defined as a person who changes their opinions or behavior according to the situation. To survive and get re-elected, the career politician must change his or her positions as frequently as the wind changes direction.

Politicians, lobbyists, and special interest groups continually shift positions as the prevailing winds change. This churning produces enough energy to cause a maximum-strength hurricane to develop. Big Media already is unleashing a torrential attack on our liberties and rule-of-law by closely aligning their news to support socialists' members of Congress.

The fifth column of rogue journalists serve as the mouth-piece for socialist members of Congress to advance their ideas to increase the power of the federal government. To succeed, they must undermine the Constitution, the Bill of Rights, and take away our individual freedoms.

Many theories are available through the internet about an evil cabal of billionaires holding secret meetings to determine our destiny. Nobody has been able to truly establish a formal cabal exists, but later in this book we will examine how several billionaires are using their fortunes to promote their socialist beliefs.

How did *"we the people"* let our government have so much power over our lives?

The Initial Move to Big Government

The following description of the justification for beginning the expansion of the federal government powers was extracted from the Franklin D. Roosevelt (FDR) Presidential Library and Museum website. Similar conditions exist today.

What was the Great Depression?

> The "Great Depression "was a severe, worldwide economic disintegration symbolized in the United States by the stock market crash on "Black Thursday," October 24, 1929. By the time that FDR was inaugurated president on March 4, 1933, the banking system had collapsed, nearly 25% of the labor force was unemployed, and prices and productivity had fallen to 1/3 of their 1929 levels.
>
> Reduced prices and reduced output resulted in lower incomes in wages, rents, dividends, and profits throughout the economy. Factories were shut down, farms and homes were lost to foreclosure, mills and mines were abandoned, and people went hungry. The resulting lower incomes meant the further inability of the people to spend or to save their way out of the crisis, thus perpetuating the economic slowdown in a seemingly never-ending cycle.
>
> At the height of the Depression in 1933, about 12,830,000 people (25% of the total workforce) were unemployed.
>
> Although farmers technically were not counted among the unemployed, drastic drops in farm commodity prices resulted in farmers losing their lands and homes to foreclosure. The displacement of the American workforce and farming communities caused families to split up or to migrate from their homes in search of work. "Hoovervilles," or shanty towns built of

The Roles of Big Tech, Big Media, and Big Government

packing crates, abandoned cars, and other scraps sprang up across the nation.

Residents of the Great Plains area, where the effects of the Depression were intensified by drought and dust storms, simply abandoned their farms, and headed for California in hopes of finding the "land of milk and honey." These parts of the nation became known as "the Dust Bowl." Gangs of unemployed youth, whose families could no longer support them, rode the rails as hobos in search of work. America 's unemployed citizens were on the move, but there was no place to go that offered relief from the Great Depression.

What was FDR's program to end the Great Depression?

<u>With the country sinking deeper into the Depression, the American public looked for active assistance from the federal government and grew increasingly dissatisfied with the economic policies of President Herbert Hoover.</u>

In his speech accepting the Democratic Party nomination in 1932, FDR pledged "a **New Deal** for the American people" if elected. Following his inauguration as President of the United States on March 4, 1933, FDR put his New Deal into action: an active, diverse, and innovative program of economic recovery.

In the First Hundred Days of his new administration, FDR pushed through Congress a package of legislation designed to lift the nation out of the Depression. FDR created new federal programs administered by so-called "alphabet agencies" For example, the AAA (Agricultural Adjustment Administration) stabilized farm prices and thus saved farms. The CCC (Civilian Conservation Corps) provided jobs to unemployed youths while improving the environment. The TVA (Tennessee Valley Authority) provided jobs and brought electricity to rural areas for the first time. The FERA (Federal Emergency Relief Administration) and the WPA (Works Progress Administration) provided jobs to thousands of unemployed Americans in construction and arts projects across the country.

Did the New Deal end the Great Depression?

Many of FDR's programs contributed to recovery, but total recovery did not result during the 1930s.

<u>FDR adopted the economic notion promoted by English economist John Maynard Keynes,</u> promoted the idea of expanded deficit spending to stimulate aggregate demand. The Treasury Department designed programs for public housing, slum clearance, railroad construction, and other massive public works. But these were pushed off the board by the massive public spending stimulated by World War II. It was war-related export demands (to support our allies against Nazi Germany and Japan) and expanded government spending to rebuild the U.S. military that led the economy back to full employment capacity production by 1941.

Under President Roosevelt the federal government took on many new responsibilities for the welfare of the people. The New Deal marked a new relationship between the people and the federal government, which had never existed to such a degree before.

The administration established the Social Security System, unemployment insurance and more agencies and programs designed to help Americans during times of economic hardship. Although the New Deal was criticized by many both in and out of government, and seriously challenged by the U.S. Supreme Court, it received the overwhelming support of the people. Franklin D. Roosevelt was the only president in U.S. history to be elected for four terms of office.[63]

FDR's Programs were the beginning of Big Government.

The degree of pain, hunger, and depression the American people experienced from 1929 to 1939 was extreme. Millions cried out for the government to intervene and solve the problems. FDR was an eloquent orator and in radio "fireside chats" with the American people convinced them the nation was in desperate times and justified his plans to expand the role of the federal government in their lives. FDR initiated the programs that changed our type of government into a socialistic democracy.

The passage of the National Industrial Recovery Act in 1933 caused many conservatives to declare the New Deal was a form of socialism or Communism as practiced in the Soviet Union. Over the next eight years, the government instituted over fifty laws and programs which fundamentally and permanently changed the U.S. federal government by expanding its size and scope - especially its role in the economy and care of the elderly and disabled through the Social Security Act.

The New Deal programs were greeted with a series of political and judicial setbacks. Arguing that they represented an unconstitutional extension of federal authority, the conservative majority on the Supreme Court invalidated several reform initiatives like the National Recovery Administration and the Agricultural Adjustment Administration.

To protect his programs from further meddling by the Supreme Court, in 1937 President Roosevelt announced a plan to add enough liberal justices to the Court to neutralize the "obstructionist" conservatives. (Does this sound familiar to the progressives' plan in Congress today?)

> This "Court-packing" turned out to be unnecessary – soon after they caught wind of the plan, the conservative justices started voting to uphold New Deal projects – but the episode did a good deal of public-relations damage to the administration and gave ammunition to many of the president's Congressional opponents.[64]

> Most of the programs expired as the nation recovered from the Great Depression and World War II. However, the precedent was set for the Congress to inject social programs into the nation whenever a situation occurred that was deemed a national emergency.

Our nation's economic condition today – seeds are being sown for more socialistic programs.

In many respects, the current conditions of the economy are like the days of FDR. The COVID-19 pandemic sparked the most severe economic crisis since the Great Depression. COVID-19 was deemed to be a *national emergency*.

The attempts to control and eradicate COVID-19 have resulted in lawsuits fighting against government controls over the people in the U.S. The outcry from this national emergency has resulted in the loss of significant freedoms for the American people. The price of the relief efforts will burden our economy for years. Here is a brief history of the impact of this terrible disease. As you read through this section, please watch the evolving patterns and the increases in attempts to control people by the federal and state governments.

Beginning in January of 2020, executive orders were issued at the national, state, and local levels to attempt to stop the spread of the virus. As the emergency grew worse, extreme actions were authorized by Congress, intending to save our nation from potential economic collapse. The first COVID-19 Relief Bill was passed, included these major provisions:

- Provided stimulus checks of $1,200 to most Americans.
- Evictions and foreclosures were frozen if tenants stated they could not pay their rents because of COVID-19.
- State unemployment benefits were supplemented by $600 per week by the federal government.
- The small business Payroll Protection Program made "forgivable" loans available to small businesses to keep people employed. The loan did not have to be paid back when documentation was submitted verifying the employer kept a required percentage of employees on its payroll. Congress authorized a total of $669 billion to prop-up small businesses.[65]

The implementation of state and local executive orders aiming to limit the spread of the virus varied greatly by state, but here are some of the most prominent ones:

- People were required to "shelter" at home if they did not work in an essential business.

- Schools were closed and online distance learning was implemented.
- Employees could work from home if their employer permitted it.
- Unless medical reasons existed, people were directed to wear protective masks.
- Exercise social distancing by maintaining six feet between people.
- Some businesses were closed or subjected to severe operating restrictions (bars and nightclubs).
- Some public gatherings (including religious services, weddings, and funerals) were prohibited or restricted.

The Impact of the Government's War on COVID-19

COVID-19 struck the United States and the world without warning. Some federal efforts did save lives and reduced the impact on our population and economy:

- in early 2020, travel into the U.S. from China and Europe where the disease was rampant was curtailed.
- production and availability of key medical equipment like ventilators was accelerated.
- emergency hospital facilities were opened to support some of the worst-hit areas like New York City (the U.S. naval ship Comfort, and the field hospital at Javits Center).
- Operation Warp Speed was initiated which resulted in the development and distribution of three highly effective vaccines before 2020 ended – a truly remarkable accomplishment.

Congressional efforts have been a mixed bag of good and bad. The 2020 efforts aimed to quickly do something good and ensure voter approval, but were rushed and imperfect.

In 2020 and 2021, Congress passed two bills totaling $4.1 trillion responding to COVID-19 and its economic effects. The first bill, the

COVID-19 Relief Bill, totaling $2.2 trillion passed with bipartisan support and was signed by President Trump in March 2020.

The Democrats' passed legislation (signed by President Biden in March 2021) that had a $1.9 trillion price tag. It passed along party lines because Republicans opposed the provisions they said were not related to COVID-19. The Democrats included $500 million in funding for museums, arts, humanities, Amtrak, and other "pork" pet projects since they could jam it through Congress since they had control of both the House and Senate. Most adult citizens received direct payments from the U.S. Treasury of $3,200 in total.

This infusion of an unprecedented amount of cash drove up pent-up demand for consumer products. Supply of in-demand products was unable to meet these new demands. COVID-19 caused serious disruptions to the manufacturing supply chain as nations around the world ordered factories to close to stop the spread of the disease.

Next, when factories could open, low-income workers in the U.S. with state and the newly allotted federal unemployment benefits were receiving more money than if they were working. Many declined to go back to work, and this phenomenon has been carried into 2023. A national labor shortage exists today in many industries. This has forced many manufacturers and businesses to reduce hours of operations.

The competition for labor drove has driven up wages. Higher labor costs and staffing problems exacerbate the supply chain and inflation problems. The anti-fossil fuel policies of the Biden administration have caused gasoline prices to increase by over $1.00 per gallon. Trucking companies are passing these costs to consumers, which only adds to inflation.

Rising prices, known as inflation, impact the cost of living, the cost of doing business, borrowing money, mortgages, corporate, and government bond yields, and every other facet of the economy. Every American is suffering a loss of buying power. The typical American household spent $709 more per month in July 2023 than they did two years ago to buy the same goods and services, according to Moody's Analytics.[66] But inflation hits low-income families the hardest because a greater percentage of their income is eroded away at the gas pump and grocery store.

The Bipartisan Infrastructure Bill (it was touted as bipartisan, but only 19 Republicans voted for it) valued at $1.1 trillion was signed into law on November 15, 2021. The bill addresses the need to build bridges, roads, broadband internet construction, and rail and transit expansion.

The Infrastructure Investment and Jobs Act was passed on November 15, 2021, at a projected cost of $1.2 trillion. This is on top of the $5.2 trillion that has already been approved in 2020 and 2021.

Trillions of dollars that were unleashed into a recovering economy has been like pouring gasoline on a fire. It has caused rapid inflation, which is systemically destroying lower-income families.

These issues have created a divisive atmosphere in Washington and in the American public along partisan political lines. Promises of "more benefits" supposedly to be funded by the wealthy is misleading.

Lower-income families are being severely punished today by increased inflation and by the taxes and fees hidden in the legislation, like higher tobacco and gasoline taxes. The ultra-rich elites of Big Tech, Big Media, Big Government and Wall Street will mitigate the effects of higher taxes by passing their increases in corporate taxes to consumers by increasing their prices.

In attempts to lower inflation, the Federal Reserve has dramatically increased interest rates in two years from .25% to 5.5% as of September 4, 2023, the highest level in 22 years. The housing market has dramatically slowed down and some economist fear a recession, but others are optimistic it can be avoided. The economic impact is immense to our economy.

Higher interest rates dramatically affect small business owners, farmers, and the lower- and middle-class citizens. It also increases U.S. Treasury debt.

The battle lines are drawn – who will control our government? Will the blowing winds from inside the rogue fifth column succeed in pressuring Congress to pass more socialistic programs?

Big Media has partnered with members of Congress attempting to change the minds of citizens to allow the government to extend its power. When people are unemployed, the majority will have to collect unemployment insurance to buy essential food and hopefully have enough to make their housing payments. When people get desperate for food and shelter, they become angry and demand the government to intervene. Big Media will stir the "winds of social injustice" causing Americans to cry out to Congress to increase existing social programs.

Benjamin Franklin made the following quote, which describes our nation's current situation perfectly:

> "When the people find that they can vote themselves money that will herald the end of the republic."

Big Tech has supplied Big Media with the systems to capture citizen's private data needed to rapidly disseminate their agendas to their base of followers or groups they choose to target. As people's minds change to embrace socialistic changes, Big Government becomes bigger.

As the government grows, Big Brother will take over in small increments.

Are you prepared?

Do you feel hopeless?

When the world looks hopelessly in a mess, this is the scripture that comes to my mind:

> "[2]Set your mind on things above, not on things on the earth." (Colossians 3:2)

Here are a couple of my favorite quotes from Dr. Carolyn Leaf (communication pathologist, cognitive neuroscientist, and author), helpful for when the discussion or news turns to politics:

> "Reaction is the key word here. You cannot control the events or circumstances of your life, but you can control your reactions."

The Roles of Big Tech, Big Media, and Big Government

> "If you can train your mind to understand God is ultimately in control and His plan for the world and you will come to pass, then you can control your reactions."

The next chapter describes the plan to expand Big Government. These plans are setting the stage for total government control. When this happens, it won't be long before *"Big Brother Is Watching You"* signs (and their digital equivalents) can be posted like they were in Oceania in the *1984* novel.

Here are two famous Ronald Reagan quotes that are very appropriate about our Big Government:

> "The nine most terrifying words in the English language are: I'm from the Government, and I'm here to help. " Regan's speech was delivered August 12, 1986.

> "Government is not the solution to our problem, government is the problem." Quote was delivered at the State of the Union address on January 20, 1981.

Chapter 9

How Socialism Will Increase in America

The hot political winds adding fuel to the Perfect Political Storm have shifted so Big Media and liberal left-wing politicians are demanding dramatic changes that are under consideration in Congress. These changes have the potential to transform the U.S. into a democratic socialist republic.

What are the major reasons why "democratic" socialism can be expected to increase dramatically in our government?

1. Dark Money is funding the move to socialism.

The Supreme Court issued a controversial decision in a 2010 ruling in the Citizens United v. Federal Election Commission that reversed century-old campaign finance restrictions. This decision enabled corporations and other outside groups to spend unlimited funds on elections. This decision has dramatically expanded the flow of money into political campaigns at the local, state, and national level. It has had negative repercussions for American democracy and the fight against political corruption. Here is a summary from the Brennan Center.

> A conservative nonprofit group called Citizens United challenged campaign finance rules after the FEC stopped it from promoting and airing a film criticizing presidential candidate Hillary Clinton too close to the presidential primaries.

> A 5-4 majority of the Supreme Court sided with Citizens United, ruling that corporations and other outside groups can spend unlimited money on elections.

> The most significant outcome of Citizens United has been the creation of Super PACs, which empower the wealthiest donors to give huge amounts of money to shadowy nonprofits. When a nonprofit gives to a political Super PAC, the donation is in the

The Roles of Big Tech, Big Media, and Big Government

name of the nonprofit so the names of the individual donors are not revealed. Nonprofits have been designed specifically for this purpose – to shield the wealthy. This process creates what is known as *"dark money."*

A Brennan Center report by Daniel I. Weiner pointed out that a very small group of Americans now wield "more power than at any time since Watergate. This is perhaps the most troubling result of Citizens United: in a time of historic wealth inequality," wrote Weiner, "this decision has helped reinforce the growing sense that our democracy primarily serves the interests of the wealthy few, and that democratic participation for the vast majority of citizens is of relatively little value."[67]

This decision has resulted in left leaning donors giving millions of dollars they could not have given without this Supreme Court decision. These left leaning donors significantly outspend their conservative donors. Here is a startling summary from Forbes:

Billionaires and millionaires played a bigger role in the 2020 election than ever before. They donated money – lots of it. More than 200 chipped in to support their favorite presidential candidates. The top 20 collectively spent $2.3 billion. Or a little more than twice as much as Joe Biden's campaign. And just one person, Michael Bloomberg, donated more than half that sum to help elect Joe Biden. The top five were:

1. Michael Bloomberg - $1.2 billion
2. Tom Steyer - $415 million
3. Sheldon & Miriam Adelson - $218 million
4. Ken Griffin - $68 million
5. Dustin Moskovitz & Cari Tuna - $52 million (META founder and youngest megadonor)[68]

Please note the above figures do not include any monies they gave to politically active nonprofits where their donations are hidden. Some of the largest donors to liberal Democratic Super PACs are not in the above list because their money was mostly *dark*.

Hansjörg Wyss

Swiss billionaire Hansjörg Wyss has quietly become one of the most important donors to left-leaning advocacy.

While most of his recent politically oriented giving was channeled through three nonprofit funds, Mr. Wyss's organizations also directly donated tens of millions of dollars since 2016 to groups that opposed former President Donald Trump and promoted Democrats and their causes.[69]

George Soros

George Soros, 93, has donated billions of dollars of his personal wealth to liberal and anti-authoritarian causes. The Hungarian-American has also been the subject of anti-Semitic attacks and conspiracy theories for decades. Unproven allegations of Soros arranging funding to support causes he supports abound. He has been accused of paying demonstrators, flying demonstrators from city-to-city, and supporting migrant caravans coming from Central America to infiltrate our southern border.

His massive donations in local and state elections, especially for district attorney races, have overwhelmed many of the candidates who oppose his position on local law and order and to defund the police.[70] These district attorneys are now distressing their communities by intentional failure to prosecute crimes and to release dangerous criminals back into the communities.

His son, Alexander Soros is taking over his father's Open Society Foundations and will continue using it to fund their socialist causes.

2. The Democrats and Republicans are deeply divided over socialism.

Bipartisanship for members of Congress has been abandoned when it comes to passing major legislation for the good of the nation. Elected officials pursue almost exclusively the agendas of their political party.

We have now in the United States Congress multiple elected representatives, in both the Senate and House of Representatives, who are self-proclaimed Democratic socialists. Senator Bernie Sanders, and Representative Alexandria Ocasio-Cortez (AOC) are two of the more prominent ones. They openly proclaim socialism is better than our current system. To help you gauge the depth of their followers, Bernie has nearly 12 million and AOC has 8 million Twitter followers. Scores of other members support "socialist agendas," but do not openly declare they are socialists like Sanders and Ocasio-Cortez.

What has changed within the Democratic Party?

Democrats began their presidential debates in 2019, Medicare-for-all was the leading subject, with Senators Elizabeth Warren (Mass.), then-Senator Kamala D. Harris joining Bernie Sanders in advancing variants Medicare for all and lowering the age to 60. Writers on the left celebrated what they called "a progressive policy arms race" led by Warren and Sanders. But then Joe Biden, who opposed the proposal, won the nomination.

The dashing of progressive hopes for health care has not stopped the shift of the Democratic Party, and the country as a whole, to the left.

Today's 2023 Democrats are indeed more left-wing than their forebears in many ways. Biden's budget foresees record levels of federal spending and debt. He has signaled more hostility to bipartisan entitlement reform than the two previous Democratic presidents did.

A major reason moderates shunned the bill: It requires raising taxes on the middle class, as Sanders readily admits. (He says the middle class will save more on medical bills than they pay in taxes.) Biden, like the other two Democrats who have been president in the past 40 years, has ruled that out.

If they're willing to raise taxes only on a small slice of the population, Democrats might not be able to keep financing the government we have. They certainly cannot finance a European-style social democracy.[71]

Democrats now favor socialism to capitalism.

Current events are rapidly changing Americans' views on socialism. Despite initiatives that have created many socialistic programs, a majority of Americans believe in capitalism and entrepreneurship. <u>A Fox News poll showed that more Democrats favor socialism over capitalism</u>, in a sharp reversal from just a year and a half ago. Here is a reprint of the summary of the story.

> **Majority of Democratic voters now prefer socialism to capitalism, poll finds**
>
> Data for Progress conducted a national survey of likely voters. Voters were initially asked how they felt about the following ideologies: capitalism, socialism, and democratic socialism. They were then presented with descriptions of each ideology before answering the same question again. The survey finds that Democrats are the only party to hold favorable views of democratic socialism and socialism, both before and after being presented with ideology descriptions; in fact, both ideologies outpace capitalism among self-identified Democrats.
>
> Among Democrats polled, capitalism is not the top-performing political ideology. Democratic socialism holds a +35-point margin of support and socialism holds a +25-point margin of support, followed by capitalism, which has only a +3-point margin of support.[72]

3. President Biden's (and previous President's) Executive Orders are undermining the constitution and ignoring Supreme Court rulings indicative of a socialist regime.

The next tactic in the move towards socialism is to extend and overuse the power of the President. Abuse of the powers of the President through executive orders is not new, but it dramatically started increasing with Presidents Obama and Trump.

Here is a quote from Michael Barone, author of *The Almanac of American Politics*, regarding this power grab:

> "[Rule by executive order] …bypasses the deliberation, compromise, and consensus-building that are inherent to legislating. Each new president now commences his term by signing orders to undo much of what his predecessor leaves behind. The fixation on executive orders contributes to a zero-

sum mindset in American politics, with each party determined not merely to advance its political agenda but also to eradicate the agenda of the other party. Executive orders are canceled as easily as they were created. Shifts in policy last for a very short time."

It took Barack Obama seven years to go from his statement "A president is not above the law" to "We're not just going to be waiting for legislation … I've got a pen and I've got a phone." Joe Biden did it in just three months.

In October 2020, candidate Biden explained, "You can't legislate by executive order unless you're a dictator." Three months later, he was sworn in as president and his actions have contradicted his earlier statement. President Biden issued 29 executive actions within three days of taking office. In his first 100 days as president, Biden issued more than 100 executive orders, proclamations, memoranda, and other executive actions.

This was a display of executive unilateralism that would make even President Obama blush. His supply of ink pens seems to be unending. For reference, as of April 29, 2021 Biden had issued 41 executive orders, more than twice the number issued by either Obama (19) or Bush (11), and two-thirds more than Trump (25) for the comparable period.

Under Article II of the Constitution, the president's authority to issue executive orders must come either from a power granted to him by the Constitution or by a law passed by Congress. The President can wield only the power he already has. He cannot give himself new powers, such as the legislative powers reserved to Congress in Article I of the Constitution. When the President exceeds his authority by legislating via executive action, he violates the fundamental system of checks and balances embedded in our constitutional form of government.[73]

Biden's orders ranged from increasing regulations, changing immigration laws, canceling contracts to *build the wall*, lifting travel bans (including nations with high terrorist risk concerns), and many more. Judicial scholars will argue many of these orders violate the President's authority (this same rationale also applies to some of the executive orders by former Presidents Clinton, Bush, Obama, and Trump).

President Biden authorized the Centers for Disease Control (CDC) to impose a nationwide temporary federal moratorium on residential evictions for nonpayment of rent. The stated purpose of the order was to prevent the further spread of COVID-19, specifically by preventing homelessness and overcrowded housing conditions resulting from eviction.

The action, which followed an Executive Order directing the CDC to consider such a measure, is unprecedented, both in terms of the federal reach into what is traditionally state and local governance of landlord-tenant law and its use of a public health authority for this purpose. Numerous lawsuits filed by landlords in attempts to recover damages from loss of income are still working their way through the courts.

The Alabama Association of Realtors challenged the Executive Order, and it went to the Supreme Court. The Court ruled that the Centers for Disease Control and Prevention exceeded its authority in continuing a moratorium on evictions after Congress failed to pass new legislation. However, the Supreme Court permitted the CDC order to continue with a warning they exceeded their authority since it had only a few weeks left before it was to expire.

President Biden ignored the Court ruling and his administration attempted a work-around based on the need to stop the spread of COVID-19. The CDC issued an extension of the moratorium ignoring the Court decision. This was a clear and blatant abuse of power.

This CDC extension order was appealed to the Supreme Court. The majority opinion of the Supreme Court states, "If a federally imposed eviction moratorium is to continue, Congress must specifically authorize it."[74] The CDC unjustly tried to impose its power, but was overruled by the court.

Here is another lawsuit that is headed to the Supreme Court after being rejected in a Federal Court. The National Apartment Association (NAA), a trade group whose members control about 10 million rental units, filed the suit in the U.S. Court of Federal Claims in Washington, D.C. The NAA claims that the CDC's Prevention eviction moratorium was unlawful and has left landlords "holding the bag on $26.6 billion in rental debt after operating under extreme conditions for 16 months," according to its announcement.[75]

The ruling on this case may be appealed, but it is an astounding ruling to dismiss this case. On May 17, 2023, Judge Bonilla's decision to dismiss the case cited cases that claim must result from "lawful" government action. Since the U.S. Supreme Court observed that the CDC's actions exceeded its authority, the moratorium was not a lawful action so that damages are not compensable under the takings clause. Essentially, a loss due to illegal government activity will not be compensated but a loss due to legal misconduct can be compensated.

Does this sound fair to you?

If the Supreme Court agrees to hear this case, an additional ruling will possibly help clarify the power states have to control commerce in times of national emergencies.

The interaction between the President and CDC and the Supreme Court highlights a critical concern. If more deadly strands of COVID-19 or another disease should materialize, will these Executive branch actions be repeated? Will federal agencies issue orders even after the Supreme Court states they have exceeded their authority?

Another Biden action that has gone to the Supreme Court tested the power of the president. In September 2021, President Biden instructed Occupational Safety and Health Administration (OSHA) to use workplace safety laws and enforce mandatory COVID-19 vaccination requirements for many employers.

The Supreme Court ruling on evictions defined the role federal agencies can take when responding to a national emergency. As of now, the authority rests in Congress, not agencies like the CDC. However, OSHA has the power to dictate workplace environments.

The Supreme Court on January 25, 2022 blocked the rules saying OSHA had exceeded the authority given to the agency by Congress.

In many states, the governor issued executive orders forcing mandatory closings or placing severe operating restrictions upon businesses and organizations that the governor deemed to be "non-essential." These state mandates destroyed thousands of small businesses and their owner's dreams and financial investments – with minimal hopes of legal recourse for recovery of their money, hopes, and dreams.

These actions sometimes reflected the political views of the governor, e.g., churches were restricted while abortion clinics, liquor stores, and pot shops were called "essential;" but weddings, funerals and family gatherings were restricted.

The number of permanent business closures was estimated at roughly 200,000 U.S. according to a study released by economists at the Federal Reserve in April 2021.[76] That number has continued to grow. Vice-President Harris stated in an interview on MSNBC on June 1, 2021, "Sadly, during the course of the pandemic, one-third of our small businesses have closed."[77]

There is no question that federal, state, and municipal governments have the power to regulate business. The so-called police power is exercised in a multitude of forms and is essential in maintaining the order that allows businesses to operate in the first place. But the Fifth and Fourteenth Amendments to the U.S. Constitution contain due process protections that prevent the federal and state governments from taking private property for public use without "just compensation." And the First Amendment to the Constitution contains protection for the 'free exercise of religion' and "freedom of speech."

So far, legal opinions regarding the COVID-19 pandemic and regulatory mandates suggest that businesses may have difficulty in succeeding in a claim they are due "just compensation." Some lawyers now are willing to argue that when a state's order was extended to an unreasonable time frame, it posed an existential threat to the continuation of a business, then financial relief from the courts should be pursued.

My comment is "good luck in suing any state government." After losing their businesses, the great majority of the owners will not have the financial strength to enter a prolonged and costly court fight with state governments.

In late 2020, the Supreme court issued decisions regarding state restrictions on church services during the pandemic where the states appeared to discriminate against churches as compared to other organizations and businesses. Generally, these were victories for religious freedom and defeats for government overreach.

Why are these cases important to you?

These executive actions should prove to you the government will do whatever it deems appropriate regardless of the damage it does to a subset of citizens or their constitutional rights. This should be our great concern to every freedom loving American. Thank God the Supreme Court has ruled against some of the Executive overreach!

4. The next move to socialism comes from the adoption of globalism.

According to the Oxford American Dictionary, globalism is the advocacy of *"the interpretation or planning of economic and foreign policy in relation to events and developments throughout the world."* In its most extreme forms, it is sometimes expressed using terms such as *"one-world,"* support for a single-world government, and/or terms such as *"world-citizen"* or *"global-citizen."*

Globalism also involves the theory of a *"global economy"* which includes all economic activities which are conducted both within and between nations, including production, consumption, economic management, exchange of financial values, and trade of goods and services. This is possible because of recent technological inventions such as the internet. Globalism and nationalism are contradictory.

- Globalists oppose nationalism, national sovereignty, and self-governance.
- Globalists point to nationalists as being racists and bigots.

Summary of the History of Globalism and Socialism

Since the time of Karl Marx, there has been a continuing effort by the left to gain power, with the goal of a worldwide socialist utopia with centralized government involved in almost all aspects of life. This push has been resisted by those who seek to maintain the more traditional structures for social structure and government

Far-left and far-right countries have this in common: they require a tyrannical centralized government to hang onto control, suppress dissent and ration the fruits of their economies to the population. Though they may claim equality and unity, and may even have "elections," there is always a small group with all the power, supported by "elite" friends, with the mass of population under their thumb. Their elections are mostly a sham.

These nations identify internal and external "enemies" as targets of blame, since these centrally governed tyrannies never function well; this often leads to war, genocide, exile, and brutality. They also seek to eliminate any opposition that may come from religion

In the first half of the 20th century, there were several "far right" nations (Germany under Hitler, Spain under Franco, Argentina under Peronist, and Italy under Mussolini). The totalitarian German and Italian states were defeated in war; Franco and Peron died in office. The cold war brought about the demise of communism in the former Soviet bloc countries.

America's population has historically fallen largely in that traditionalist political center range. The U.S. Constitution includes various safety valves and trip levers built to avoid sudden radical shifts to either the left or right.

In the early 1900's and during the Great Depression, there were pushes for communism. The pushes included riots, bombings, and some domestic terrorism, but did not gain broad popular support. That did not deter the left, they have just revised their strategies. There have been some small far right movements in the United States, but these went nowhere. Far right groups in America are now small groups on the fringe of politics even though the left points to them as the bogeymen when they need an enemy to blame or target.

The American population still falls mostly in that broad center range of people who just want to live their lives with friends and family and leave things better than they found them. In the 20th Century, some good things came from the efforts of liberals - the end of segregation and advances in civil rights. Conservatives gave us a stronger economy, lower taxes, and healthy employment conditions.

A populist movement early in the 20th century busted the big business monopolies, trusts, and oligopolies and established essential protection for workers and consumers. Liberals and conservatives cooperated for the good of the country, enabling American victories in World Wars I and II and the Cold War. They also passed environmental laws for cleaner air and water. At times, this cooperation, compromise, and success seemed too good to be true.

Twentieth-century politics were mostly defined by economic issues. On the left, politics centered on workers, trade unions, and social welfare programs. Conservatives on the right were primarily interested in reducing the size of government and promoting the private sector and jobs.

When Jimmy Carter became president, things started to unravel for the left. The country's economy faltered as inflation soared, interest and unemployment rates skyrocketed, and there were gas shortages. The failings of leftist economic policies were too visible to every citizen. Also, there were too many examples here in the U.S. of everyday people achieving economic success through creativity and hard work. Ronald Reagan was elected President in a landslide, as the nation's voters called for a change in direction. The left realized their focus on the "economic class struggle" wasn't working. They needed a better way to create divisive conflicts in the U.S.

Are we seeing history repeat itself under President Biden?

The left's strategy has added to its economic concerns for the poor and middle class a major emphasis upon questions of "identity politics." The left has prioritized issues coming from activists in a wide variety of marginalized groups, e.g., ethnic minorities, immigrants and refugees, transgender and LGBTQ groups. They want to solidify these groups as part of their base.

Today, identity politics has become a master concept that explains much of what is going on in American politics and in global affairs.

Power for the left depends on the creation of internal conflicts that fracture society. For many decades (dating back at least as far as Karl Marx) the left promoted political struggles as a reflection of economic conflicts. This conflict was successfully exploited by the communists in the overthrow of governments in Russia and China.

Today, all over the world, political leaders have mobilized followers based on the idea that their dignity has been affronted and must be restored. Resentment over indignities has become a powerful force. The Black Lives Matter movement sprang from a series of a few well-publicized police killings of African Americans. The BLM movement (and Big Media) forced the rest of the world to pay attention while ignoring the growing numbers of people murdered by criminals in big cities and line-of-duty police deaths.

On college campuses and in offices around the U.S., women were infuriated over an epidemic of sexual harassments and assaults perpetrated by people in power and the lack of consequences for the perpetrators. The issues of transgender people, a tiny group who had previously not been widely recognized as distinct targets of discrimination, became a cause célèbre.

Transgender men have begun dominating women's sports. NCAA swimmer Riley Gaines was tied by Lia Thomas, a transgender athlete, in the 2022 championship. That changed everything for Gaines. Gaines began a nationwide campaign opposing transgender women competing against biological females. She says her goals, like stopping proposed changes to Title IX, are intended to protect women's sports like swimming, tennis, track and field, and even weight lifting. Her efforts have helped 23 states to pass laws requiring transgender athletes' to take part in school sports in accordance with their birth identity.

Again and again, groups have come to believe that their identities - whether nationality, religious, ethnic, sexual, gender, or otherwise - are not receiving adequate recognition. Identity politics is no longer a minor phenomenon, playing out only in the rarified confines of university campuses or providing a backdrop to low-stakes skirmishes in "culture wars" promoted by the mass media. Instead, identity politics has become a master concept that explains much of what is going on in America today.[78]

Critical Race Theory (CRT) is causing white people to find themselves being identified as being the oppressor for one or more of these groups, or are inappropriately described having some privilege despite never actually having done anything. These ordinary people find themselves labeled as "racists, fascists or Nazi's." They are told they must make restitution or be punished for some historical grievance. Some are puzzled or confused about how this can be happening in America. Others point out that these arguments are the re-embodiment of the old racism that America thought to have ended because of the Civil Rights movement and legislation in the 1960's.

Another new development in identity politics is progressive blue states issuing boycotts preventing travel or the purchase of select products from red states because they disagree with the red states political agendas. California began in 2017 enforcing a new law that was passed that has been extended to ban state-funded travel to Alabama, Florida, Idaho, Iowa, Kansas, Kentucky, Mississippi, North Carolina, Oklahoma, South Carolina, South Dakota, Tennessee, and Texas. California asserts these states support or finance discrimination against lesbian, gay, bisexual, and transgender because the laws of these states adversely target these groups. The city of Portland, Oregon plans to boycott Texas goods and services over the new Texas law limiting abortions.

Ironically, many people are now avoiding California and Portland (once considered friendly and picturesque) due to the rampant violent crime and urban decay that has been produced by long term progressive control of both California and Oregon.

"The Great Reset" and Globalism

The Great Reset is an important part of the Globalist agenda that has a profound influence on the minds of people and is being widely endorsed by our progressive politicians and by some Republicans owing allegiance to big multinational corporations. The Great Reset is the beginning of the end for our founding fathers' plan for our nation, if it is implemented. The move coincides with the fact we are rapidly moving into End Time events and the Great Reset is part of Satan's plan to achieve his one-world government.

The Great Reset was the name of the 50th annual meeting of the World Economic Forum (WEF), held in June 2020 in Davos, Switzerland. It brought together high-profile business and political leaders who convened with the theme of how to rebuild society and the economy in a "more sustainable way" based on environmental, social, and governance metrics which would incorporate more "green" public infrastructure projects.

The COVID-19 pandemic has presented an opportunity to formulate an economic recovery that will produce a "new capitalism," that is not really capitalism at all. This, in turn, would produce global monetary controls, and an international socialist system![79]

Joe Biden's campaign to "Build Back Better" plan comes straight from the Great Reset's playbook. Great Reset supporters, especially the World Economic Forum (WEF), have been calling for some variation of a "Build Back Better" plan for years, often using those exact words in WEF materials. In fact, as recently as July 13, 2020 the World Economic Forum promoted "building back better" through "green" infrastructure programs as part of the Great Reset in an article titled *"To build back better, we must reinvent capitalism."*

Because of COVID, the WEF resumed meeting in January 2023 with 2,500 attendees. These world leaders and experts addressed the most pressing challenges of our time:

- The Russia - Ukraine war.
- The future of the global world order.
- The growing urgency of the climate crisis and its impact on food and poverty.
- The outlook for a future recession.
- How to end COVID-19 and prepare for the next pandemic when many countries still don't have access to vaccines.

Does this sound like a diabolical plan to move the world to a one-world government?

5. The government is unlawfully monitoring and surveilling you as if we live in a socialist nation.

The U.S. Foreign Intelligence Surveillance Court (FISC, also called the FISA Court) is a U.S. federal court established under the Foreign Intelligence Surveillance Act of 1978 (FISA) to oversee requests for surveillance warrants against foreign spies inside the U.S. by federal law enforcement and intelligence agencies. The FISA court has a long history of abuses.

In 2013, a top-secret order issued by the court, which was later leaked to the media from documents by Edward Snowden, required a subsidiary of Verizon to provide a daily, ongoing feed of all call detail records – including those for domestic calls – to the NSA. The scandal broke in early June 2013 when the Guardian newspaper reported that the U.S. National Security Agency (NSA) was collecting the telephone records of tens of millions of Americans.

That report was followed by revelations in both the Washington Post and Guardian that the NSA tapped directly into the servers of nine internet firms, including META, Google, Microsoft, and Yahoo to track online communication in a surveillance program known as Prism. Documents leaked to the Washington Post suggested the NSA breaks U.S. privacy laws hundreds of times every year.

The outcry from Congress was loud, political, and action was demanded to ensure not just the NSA, but all government agencies protected the rights of citizens. However, Snowden's leaks resulted in just one new law, which is an attempt to end the NSA's bulk collection of Americans' phone records.

The new law now requires the NSA to go to private phone companies when seeking data. Under the previous system, the NSA reportedly had trouble acquiring records from cell phones. Now it can obtain them with a court order. The records detail the numbers involved in a phone call, when it occurred and how long it lasted, but do not include the content of the conversations. Congress ended up expanding the amount of information available to the spy agency.

The collection, distribution and use of cell phone data and another indication Big Brother is coming. The following article is alarming.

On February 7, 2020, the Wall Street Journal reported about U.S. government purchase and use of certain cell phone location data for law enforcement purposes during 2017-2019.

Federal Agencies Use Cell Phone Location Data for Immigration Enforcement

The Trump administration bought access to a commercial database that maps the movements of millions of cell phones in America to use it for immigration and border enforcement, according to people familiar with the matter and documents reviewed by The Wall Street Journal. The location data is drawn from ordinary cell phone apps, including those for games, weather, and e-commerce, for which the user has granted permission to log the phone's location.

The Department of Homeland Security has used the information to detect undocumented immigrants and others who may be entering the U.S. unlawfully, according to these sources and documents. U.S. Immigration and Customs Enforcement, a division of DHS, has used the data to help identify immigrants who were later arrested. U.S. Customs and Border Protection, another agency under DHS, uses the information to look for cell phone activity in unusual places, such as remote stretches of desert that straddle the Mexican border.

The federal government's use of such data for law enforcement purposes hasn't previously been reported. Experts say the information amounts to one of the largest known troves of bulk data being deployed by law enforcement in the U.S.—and that the use appears to be on firm legal footing because the government buys access to it from a commercial vendor, just as a private company could, though its use hasn't been tested in court.

"**This is a classic situation where creeping commercial surveillance in the private sector is now bleeding directly over into government,**" said Alan Butler, general counsel of the Electronic Privacy Information Center, a think tank that pushes for stronger privacy laws. **[bold emphasis added]**

The Department of Homeland Security acknowledged buying access to the data, but wouldn't discuss details about how they are using it in law-enforcement operations.[80]

The ACLU soon requested more information using the Freedom of Information Act from the federal authorities about this program. In December 2020, the ACLU sued to speed up the answer to this request.

We might appreciate efforts to prevent drug smuggling into the U.S. We might want to stop the tidal wave of immigrants that has swept over our southern border since the 2021 Biden inauguration. In that context, this might seem like an appropriate government use of commercially available information.

But, the ease with which this program was implemented under President Trump without public awareness should give us great concern. What would prevent another administration from implementing a similar program for the purpose of tracking its political opponents? What would prevent tracking of people who attend church regularly on Sunday mornings, or those who attend political rallies?

Wiretaps

The Department of Justice's internal watchdog has found "apparent errors or inadequately supported facts" in more than two dozen FBI wiretap applications to the secretive domestic surveillance court. Those findings come from an initial audit by Justice Department Inspector General Michael Horowitz of 29 FBI applications to the FISA court.

They point to widespread problems with the bureau's handling of national security surveillance warrants beyond the recent highly charged case of former Trump campaign adviser Carter Page. That report identified 17 significant errors or omissions in the bureau's application to the FISA Court to wiretap Page.

In addition to errors and omissions, Kevin Clinesmith, a former FBI lawyer, admitted in a plea bargain deal with prosecutors that he had altered an internal FBI email in a claim presented to the FISA court to sustain government surveillance on Carter Page.

Are you convinced our government surveillance is out of control despite efforts to reel it in?

The black budget can be complicated to calculate, but in the United States it has been estimated to be over $50 billion a year, taking up approximately 7 percent of the U.S. American defense budget.[81] Does this make you uncomfortable that our intelligence agencies are getting enormous amounts of money to enhance both military and civil spying capabilities? Yet, we have no knowledge of what they are developing and how it is being implemented.

The Perfect Political Storm

The damage and results from the Perfect Political Storm have been presented. It is a continuing storm increasing in strength and it has the potential to destroy, or at a minimum make the U.S. a deeply in-debt socialist democracy. With the current debt, and excluding the passage of any new legislation, by the year 2030, debt interest payments are projected to be $665 billion and consume 10% of the total government revenue.[82]

If inflation continues, and interest rates increase or remain at current levels for an extended time, the debt service would be greater than 10% of revenues. The current national debt is $32 trillion with Congress seeking to add more. <u>In 1985, the U.S. went from no debt in 1984 to $1.8 billion in 1985.</u> It is incredible how fast and loose politicians have been with our money.

Each of these developments in our government are troubling. My personal belief is when the Supreme Court began making decisions to remove God as the source of strength for our nation, our troubles intensified.

"GOD BLESS AMERICA!" is enthusiastically sung by the vast majority of Americans. We all want "God" to bless America, but when being sung, not everyone agrees on the meaning of the phrase. God has been banished from the so-called "public square" in American life. He has been evicted from education, from law, and from the workplace. In some schools, children are not allowed to draw a picture of the Nativity scene.

Attempts by atheists, agnostics, and humanists' groups wage a relentless battle to remove Bible verses from federal, state, municipal buildings, public parks, and monuments. The courts have consistently ruled in the favor of these anti-Christian groups.

Where is our nation headed?

Will we be enslaved to debt resulting in higher taxes and significant increases in inflation?

The Social Security Administration released in September 2021 the latest status report on its trust fund. Some experts are warning that up to 20% in payment cuts could be coming as early as 2032, unless Congress intervenes with measures to preserve funding for the program.[83]

Here is a quote that is very true and it makes me mad:

> The money that goes into Social Security is not the government's money. It's your money. You paid for it. - Mitch McConnell

Now let's move on to good news. The next chapter on Bible prophecy should clarify God's plan and provide HOPE for you and your future.

All the while, the Rapture count-down clock is ticking.

Are you watching?

Tic-Toc. Tic-Toc. Tic-Toc.

Chapter 10

Bible Prophecy

The previous chapters have described how three-headed hydra is bringing together the elements of the Perfect Political Storm. To summarize:

- Big Tech develops and supplies the tools needed by Big Media to publicize their liberal social agendas.
- Big Tech captures either legally or illegally your personal data.
- Big Tech and Big Media work in unison to promote and energize Big Government, then Big Government funds lucrative contracts to both Big Tech and Big Media.
- Collectively, the three Bigs become the Perfect Political Storm, capable of destroying the original intent of our founding fathers – life, liberty, and the pursuit of happiness.

Within a few years, our nation could be different from what our founding fathers envisioned when they adopted our Constitution and Bill of Rights. Our citizens may choose the path to destruction under progressive socialism by being like the crew of Andrea Gail in the Perfect Storm movie who hoped to save their valuable catch by sailing into the path of a powerful nor-easter, but sailed into a hurricane instead. Or, perhaps we will choose the wiser path established by our forefathers and guard our Constitution and Bill of Rights. Just like the characters in the movie, *"we the people"* will collectively decide if we want to embrace more socialism and change the course of democracy, or return to our original national course.

Regardless of which direction our nation takes, the Perfect Political Storm will seem like a mild tropical disturbance when people begin experiencing God's Ultimate Perfect Storm. To describe this storm as an ultimate hurricane using current terminology fails to provide an

The Roles of Big Tech, Big Media, and Big Government

adequate description of the horrors that begin at the start of the Tribulation. Every nation and person on earth will be impacted.

The Ultimate Perfect Storm began building with a lie from Satan.

> "³...the fruit of the tree which is in the midst of the garden, God has said, You shall not eat it, nor shall you touch it, lest you die. ⁴...You will not surely die. ⁵For God knows that in the day you eat of it your eyes will be opened, and you will be like God, knowing good and evil." (Genesis 3:4-5)

Satan's lie was the *Great Lie*. It led to the downfall of Adam and Eve and sin entered the world, and sin will remain until the End Times are completed.

God recorded for us a scripture that explains the state of the world today:

> "²⁵... [sinners] who exchanged the truth of God for the lie, and worshiped and served the creature rather than the Creator..." (Romans 1:25)

Jesus spoke about a time to come when the deception will be especially great when false messiahs and false prophets will appear. Even the people of God could be deceived if it were not for God's providential protection: "For false messiahs and false prophets will appear and perform great signs and wonders to deceive, if possible, even the elect" (Matthew 24:24, Mark 13:5–6, Luke 21:8).

No matter how powerful Big Tech, Big Media, and Big Government become, they cannot overcome human imperfection (humanity's sin nature), nor can they become like God, try as they may. The people who comprise and lead Big Tech, Big Media and Big Government all have the same human shortcomings and sin nature.

Governments cannot legislate morality through laws. We have more laws than any time in history, and progressives cry out that we have "a larger share of our population in prison than any other country in the world."[84] Instead of taming our sinful nature, laws to control our sinful nature only amplify it.

This is particularly true when the laws are selectively and unequally applied, or are not enforced at all. The current political climate and the strategies to empty prisons, defund the police, and decline prosecutions of violent criminals are providing ample evidence of the widespread failure of our legal system and the danger from politicizing the justice system.

New advances in technology are occurring at phenomenal speeds increasing tremendously the power and capabilities of the big three hydra heads. They are approaching the pinnacle of success appearing to be like God. They are like the builders of the ancient Tower of Babel, thousands of years ago. Humans began building the tower using the most advanced tools they had at the time. God said this about the people building the tower to Heaven:

> "*6...The Lord said, "If as one people speaking the same language they have begun to do this, then nothing they plan to do will be impossible for them." (Genesis 11:6)*

Big Tech's radical new technological and medical advances can result in sins of pride, arrogance, and self-exhalation because *"nothing they plan will be impossible for them."* However, God will permit these advances to continue only until the timeline to execute His final milestone in His plan for humanity arrives - The Ultimate Perfect Storm.

How do we know when the Ultimate Perfect Storm will hit?

Jesus vividly described in the Bible the End Times conditions that lead up to the next major event in God's plan to redeem humanity - the Rapture.

> "*3As he was sitting on the Mount of Olives, his disciples came to him privately. Tell us, they said, when will these things happen? And what will be the sign that you are going to appear as king, and that the end of the age is upon us?*
>
> *4And Jesus answered and said to them, See to it that no one misleads you. 5For many will come in My name, saying, I am the Christ, and will mislead many. 6You will be hearing of wars and rumors of wars. See that you are not frightened, for those things*

> must take place, but that is not yet the end. [7]*For nation will rise against nation, and kingdom against kingdom, and in various places there will be famines, pestilences, and earthquakes.* [8]*But all these things are merely the beginning of birth pangs."* (Matthew 24:3-7)

Jesus described in verse seven the conditions that will exist before the Rapture. Increases in wars, famines, diseases (pestilences), and earthquakes will occur as the Rapture gets closer. Previously, I stated my belief that Big Tech and Big Media are the *key enablers* for the signs Jesus said would come as we are approaching the *"end of the age."* Deception of the people is the key sign.

In the preceding chapters, the roles of Big Tech, Big Media, and Big Government have been explored in End Times. The following descriptions depict how their roles impact and hasten the completion of the signs Jesus described that were the beginning of the end, or were like birth pangs when a woman goes into childbirth.

Deception: Big Tech and Media deliver broadcasts with little regard to the truth – they want only to capture listeners and viewers to increase both their companies' profits, or proliferate their social and political views. Their goal is to arouse strong reactions over politics, religion, social values, police, racial inequality, etc. These emotions affect the ability of people to think rationally, and then their emotions can escalate to anger, bitterness, resentment, and finally hatred. These feelings become like a poison that destroys people from within that eats away at their hearts and minds. Then people can then turn to violence or show their anger in demonstrations that turn into riots.

Big Tech and Big Media stereotype Christians as people holding radical religious viewpoints and who will go to extremes to assert them. Christian beliefs and behaviors are presented almost always in a negative and extremist context, e.g., abortion infringes upon a woman's right of choice, or preaching against sins of homosexuality is hate speech. Satan has used deception successfully to undermine the values of Christianity. These tactics have succeeded in weakening the Christian church.

Wars and rumors of war: If you watch the news, it is filled with threats of aggression and potential (rumors) of war. Russia's invasion of Ukraine in February 2022 shocked everyone. European nations were terrified when Vladimir Putin threatened to use nuclear weapons in the war.

The most recent news revelation is that both Russia and China now have hypersonic missiles that can evade U.S. missile defenses by travelling at speeds of more than five times the speed of sound, or about 3,853 mph, making them harder to detect and intercept. Regional wars are being fought today in Syria, Yemen, Iraq, and Nigeria.

There has not been a major world war approaching the magnitude of World War II, but presently the numerous regional conflicts around the world have resulted in the deaths of an estimated 20 plus million people since 1970.[85] Terrorism continues to be a global problem, with support coming from rogue states like Iran and North Korea. China and Russia provide support for destabilization of the western democracies, push their borders and control spheres outward and threaten their neighbors. China's reclamation and re-construction of the South China Sea islands between 2013 to 2018 is a prime example of expansionism.

The disastrous American withdrawal from Afghanistan in August 2021 and the perception of weak leadership in the Biden administration may embolden these bad actors to try and take advantage of the situation. Don't be surprised if China continues to severely threaten, or even invades Taiwan. Or, if Taiwan's multi-party democracy yields to China's increasing aggression and agrees to end their sovereign nation status.

Taiwan has the world's 20th largest economy and now makes around 92% of the world's most sophisticated computer chips.[86] This capitulation would be disastrous and give China an unprecedented advantage in world trade. They could manipulate chip prices to bring world production to a standstill.

Nation against nation: In addition to nation against nation meaning war between nations, another interpretation of these words refers to fighting over racial division. Big Tech and Big Media through social and news media outlets constantly sow the seeds of racial inequality, racial divide, and provide biased reporting on *"non-violent"* social demonstrations which are violent riots resulting in millions of dollars in damages. Many public schools and colleges are teaching Critical Race Theory which has become a major factor in creating racial division.

Famines: In the past few decades, Big Tech's agricultural scientists have developed hybrid plants that have improved crop yields resulting in increased global food production supplies at a faster rate than population growth. Sadly, this has not ended hunger around the world. Uneven distribution (often caused by political forces, conflicts, and greed) results in hunger and malnutrition. Progressive activists are using Big Media as a platform to "save the planet" by attempting to block the use of modern farming tools in the underdeveloped world, such as fossil-fuel powered farm machinery and the use of fertilizer and pesticides.

Despite the technological advances in transportation, breakdowns in the food supply chain result in food not being delivered to the people who most need it. From 2019 to 2020, the number of undernourished people grew by 161 million, a crisis driven largely by conflict, drought, and the COVID-19 pandemic.[87]

Pestilence: Several severe and deadly diseases have come into existence in the last thirty years, e.g., Ebola (1976), AIDS (1981), and COVID-19 (2020). Thus far, by the mercy of God and medical science, none of these has produced a massive global death toll like the Spanish Flu in 1918 (where an estimated 50 million people died).[88] But the risk of new deadly diseases and variants has increased from the efforts in some nations to develop biological weapons. The efforts to weaponize diseases are being done in third-world countries with labs that have inadequate safety protocols.

COVID-19 is a disease or pestilence that caught the world by surprise and has been a major catastrophic event. Increasing evidence is emerging that it was a man-made disease developed in Wuhan, China. Many authorities believe it may have been developed as part of a biological warfare experiment. Perhaps time will reveal the truth, but it is doubtful the truth will ever be known since China has refused access to the lab in Wuhan. Expectations from existing scientists are that more variants of COVID-19 will mutate and have the potential to be more deadly.

Earthquakes and volcanoes:

There is new evidence the number of larger earthquakes is increasing. Analysis of seismic activity by Rystad Energy reveals that tremors of above the magnitude of 2 on the Richter scale quadrupled in 2020 and are on track to increase even further in frequency in 2021.[89] Earthquakes often are accompanied by their lethal sisters - tsunamis and volcanic eruptions.

The number of larger earthquakes is increasing. Volcanologists believe the *big one* is inevitable and that it has the potential to devastate the earth. In the year 2022, over 11 earthquakes of 7.0 magnitude happened, and in the first half of 2023 over 100 quakes occurred that had an intensity between 6.0 and 6.9.[90] The massive earthquake that hit Turkey and Syria in February 2023 killed over fifty thousand people and had a magnitude of 7.8 on the Richter scale. Five earthquakes of a magnitude between 7.0 and 7.9 shook the area in February 2023.[91]

Big Tech and Big Media are key enablers to intensify the events Jesus described.

They are the catalysts expediting the advance of each of these major signs.

As previously discussed, the rebirth of the nation of Israel triggered the End Times countdown. Bible scholars are in general agreement that we are in the very last years of this countdown. For a complete discussion on this topic, please consider reading my book *The Date of the Rapture*. It gives a *possible* date based upon the Levitical feasts the Jews were instructed to honor ancient Jewish teachings that humanity has a 6,000-year life cycle divided into three 2,000 segments. We are clearly in the last 2,000 years, and closer to the end than most people think!

Next, what will be the single event that signals the beginning of the end of the End Times?

For believers in Jesus, it is the long-awaited Rapture. For non-believers, it is the beginning of their worst possible nightmare. The non-believers will be *left behind* on earth to endure seven years of death and destruction.

Before the Tribulation begins, a cataclysmic event must occur to produce a seven-year peace agreement between Israel and its Arab neighbors. The Ezekiel 38 War, described by the Bible in Ezekiel 38 and 39, will probably be the event.

The details of this war were written over 2,500 years ago and it is the only instance in the Bible where the names of the countries are spelled out in advance of a war. Iran, Syria, Libya, and Russia come together to attack Israel, and Ezekiel declares the war only lasts one day.

Israel's victory in this war will encourage the Jews, seeing that God has won the day and glorified Himself as He did in ancient times against the Pharaoh of Egypt (Ezekiel 38:23). They will believe God has intervened for them since they are His chosen people. The Jews will be euphoric and will celebrate their Fall feasts in glorious fashion.

Through the prophet Ezekiel, God describes how these nations will plot, prepare, and come to attack Israel. Perhaps Israel will defend itself by using a dramatic weapon. Israel is believed to have several dozen atomic bombs and will probably use them.

The belief that atomic bombs will be used comes from a description of this war in Ezekiel. It states that God will respond with hot anger by unleashing a great earthquake, causing the attackers to turn their weapons on each other, pour down torrents of rain, hailstones and burning sulfur, and bring plague upon them Ezekiel (38:18-39:16).

Most scholars interpret this passage to describe the use of modern-day nuclear weapons. However, the Old Testament records several times in history where God used supernatural forces to destroy the enemies of Israel (Exodus 14:26-28, Joshua 10:10-20, 2 Kings 19:35-36, and 2 Chronicles 20:22-24).

The world, including Israel's allies, will be severely traumatized by this one-day war. The Arab nations and Russia will be in shock and total defeat. By this point, the Antichrist will probably have a major role in European politics - likely as the head of the European Union. Immediately after the war, he successfully negotiates a seven-year peace treaty with Israel and accelerates his rise to worldwide prominence and power.

The Rapture happens either right before or immediately after the war. It is God's vehicle to remove the believers in Jesus to a place of safety and beauty, prior to the horrific period of the Tribulation.

> "[52]in a flash, in the twinkling of an eye, at the last trumpet. For the trumpet will sound, the dead will be raised imperishable, and we will be changed." (1 Corinthians 15:52)

> "[16]For the Lord himself will come down from heaven, with a loud command, with the voice of the archangel and with the trumpet call of God, and the dead in Christ will rise first. [17]After that, we who are still alive and are left will be caught up together with them in the clouds to meet the Lord in the air. And so, we will be with the Lord forever. [18]Therefore encourage one another with these words." (1 Thessalonians 4:16-18)

At first, the Jews will not understand the Rapture. Many will try to rationalize why so many people disappeared. But, during the Tribulation, God will send two special messengers to teach the truth to the Jewish people and the rest of the world, though most people will not accept and believe the message. God will also anoint 144,000 Jewish evangelists that to share the good news Jesus offers salvation to all.

The peace treaty with the Antichrist will enable the nation of Israel to live in relative peace for the first three and one-half years of the Tribulation. The Jews and the people who become Christians in the

Tribulation are still endangered by most of the judgments unleashed during the Tribulation and from the relentless persecution from the Antichrist. Midway through the seven years, the Antichrist breaks his peace treaty, and begins a drive to annihilate the Jewish people.

The Day of The Lord

The Day of the Lord describes the series of events by which Jesus gives the final call to believe in Him, brings judgment upon sin, and brings about a perfect eternal state. It includes the Tribulation, His Second Coming, the Millennial Kingdom, the Great White Throne Judgment, and the establishment of the New Heaven and New Earth. It is a time of judgment, destruction, and punishment. But it is also His final call to humanity, "Accept the gift of eternal life through My Son, Jesus Christ, or face eternal punishment and separation from Me."

During the Day of the Lord, God will end all oppression, corruption, sin, and evil on earth. The Day of the Lord includes these periods:

- The seven years of the Tribulation will be ended by Christ's complete victory at the Battle of Armageddon. The Antichrist and his false prophet sidekick are thrown into the lake of fire; followed by

- The thousand years of the Millennial Kingdom, where Christ will rule perfectly and fulfill all the Bible's promises to the Jewish nation. After one thousand years, the final judgment occurs.

- The Great White Throne Judgment is where Christ sits on the throne as judge. If a person's name is not recorded in Christ's *Book of Life*, that person is already guilty. This judgment is a sentencing hearing. All unbelievers are condemned to eternal punishment in the lake of fire joining Satan, the Antichrist, false prophet, and all of the fallen angels.

The Great White Throne Judgment is followed by the establishment of the eternal state called Eternity, ruled by King Jesus. God will be with his people and He will live with them.

Why is the Tribulation the Ultimate Perfect Storm?

The Tribulation will be a time of punishment, terrible plagues, famine, disaster, and the darkest times in human history.

During this era, Jesus will unleash twenty-one plagues, natural disasters, and supernatural events of unprecedented severity to get people's attention, pointing out their rejection of God. The people will have an opportunity to repent and become believers in Jesus. Millions of people will do so but, unfortunately, most people will not. These judgments are specific, horrible, and result in the death of about two-thirds of the world's population – 5 to 6 billion people die.

The fury of the worst imaginable hurricane is absolutely nothing compared to the fury that will occur during the Tribulation period and the eternal punishment that unbelievers will face after being judged at the Great White Throne.

Do these prophecies cause you to think about where the world is headed?

Have you given any thought about watching for the Rapture? When it comes, will you be taken up with Jesus, or will you be left behind for the Tribulation? Will your name be found in Christ's *Book of Life*?

> *"[44]Therefore you also <u>be ready</u>, for the Son of Man is coming at an hour you do not expect." (Matthew 24:44)*

The Rapture count-down clock is running down.

Tic-Toc, Tic-Toc, Tic-Toc...

Chapter 11

Closing Comments

We have become accustomed to the products and services that Big Tech delivers to make our lives comfortable and enjoyable. Big Media is a self-appointed prophet, proclaiming the altruistic goal of nirvana on earth for the poor and oppressed with utopian fairness for everyone. Big Government's politicians will continue to strive to follow the changing winds of public opinion, heed the wishes of the elites (in politics, academia, and finance) while listening to the hot air from Big Media.

Here is an appropriate scripture that describes the U.S. today.

> "[37]But as the days of Noah were, so also will the coming of the Son of Man be. [38]For as in the days before the flood, they were eating and drinking, marrying and giving in marriage, until the day that Noah entered the ark." (Matthew 24:37-38)

The ark in the scripture above is a symbol representing the Rapture. The Rapture will enable true believers to escape going through the Ultimate Perfect Storm – The Tribulation. We are very near to the Rapture.

Our government has tools to influence in ways the world has never known before, from mass communication resources to faceless computerized bureaucracies. These tools instead of being used for good are being used for evil. The Perfect Political Storm is raging as the influence of Big Tech, Big Media, and Big Government converge.

Our nation is being torn apart by racial strife, bigotry, and hate. We are going down a dangerous path where "hate crime" charges and punishment are applied to frustrate free speech and religious truth, which is now called "hate speech, and thus our First Amendment rights are curtailed. This will continue as the media and government try to manipulate us and invoke greater control.

Satan was right when he said:

"*²All that a man has he will give for his life.*" *(Job 2:4)*

If the citizens of America become convinced that the government can guarantee their financial future with free benefits, they are likely to support and obey that government, unless someone shows them that they are being led down a very dangerous path.

Unfortunately, given a choice, many people would prefer economic equality with tyranny rather than economic opportunity with freedom. In free societies, all outcomes are not guaranteed to be economically equal, even if given equal opportunities.

When the Antichrist assumes power, he will use the legal system and governmental forces to prosecute and punish those who do not worship him. Daniel 7:25 says that he will *"change the times and the law."* Liberal activists are already attempting to change our laws, but this is only the beginning. It is going to get much worse.

Will we say good-by to our freedoms?

Will the socialist agendas come to fruition?

These are perplexing questions. I don't have the answers, but the signs of God's plan continue to unfold before our eyes. Many believers are in awe as they discern that the long-awaited Rapture, prophesied thousands of years ago, will probably happen in most of our lifetimes.

Technology is rapidly advancing the capability so our government can have control over Americans. Increasingly, warning signs saying "Big Brother Is Watching You" might appear on your electronic devices and around your neighborhood.

Can you see where we are headed? It is not a matter of ***if***, but rather of ***when*** it will happen. And it will probably be sooner than we think.

There is good news in this. As many prophecy teachers acknowledge, **"things are not falling apart, but they are falling into place."**

What do we do as Christians?

The Roles of Big Tech, Big Media, and Big Government

The following are some paraphrased thoughts from a great book I highly recommend, *When a Nation Forgets God* by Erwin Lutzer, pastor emeritus of The Moody Church in Chicago, where he served 36 years as the senior pastor.

> When confronted with these challenges, we are tempted to do the wrong thing—to react with judgmental anger that will only entrench those who are on the other side in this culture war. We must do the opposite: to respond with humility and gracious courage. We will neither win these battles simply with politics, nor by argument. Every Christian must regain the high ground with credibility, virtue, and yes, with joy. We must stand our ground giving thanks to God, even as it shifts beneath our feet. We dare not give to Caesar that which is God's.
>
> Believers cannot choose to remain silent about preaching the gospel. Sharing the gospel is, of course, our primary responsibility since it is only the cross of Christ that can transform the human heart. But once we have received the gift of salvation through Christ, we must live out the implications of the cross in every area of our life. We must be prepared to submit to the Lordship of Christ in all "spheres." Here in America, we must respond to our own challenges on multiple levels.
>
> We must educate our citizenry on both our history and what is taking place in our government, courts, and schools. We must do our homework in knowing what our politicians believe about these issues and be sure to vote for those who are most compatible with our values. Then we must also support organizations that are working to preserve our freedoms, such as the National Religious Broadcasters in Washington (www.nrb.org), which is dedicated to keeping media outlets free of government interference for the proclamation of the gospel. Finally, we must strengthen individual believers in our churches for the ominous days ahead.
>
> The conflict is really between humanism and Christianity; or alternative religions and Christianity. On one side is a deteriorating culture and on the other side of the divide is the cross of Christ with its message of hope and redemption. For us

as Christians it is really a struggle for the survival of the message of the cross in our increasingly hostile culture. If ever Christians need to be sharing the message of the gospel, "which is the power of God unto salvation," it is now.

Have we forgotten that God's power is more clearly seen in the message of the cross than in any political or social plan we might devise?

What, after all, is the meaning of the cross about which we speak? Why should Christians "cling to the old rugged cross," as the old hymn reminds us to do? Surely, we might think we have outgrown such sentimentality. But it is exactly here that Christianity stands or falls; it is the meaning of the cross that gives Christianity its power.

The cross exposes the futility of all our self-righteousness; it reminds us that we are sinners incapable of bringing about our own reconciliation with God. Christ died to save sinners, to reveal the love of God, and to conquer evil. Before this cross we can only stand with bowed heads and broken spirits.

At what point do we have to become lawbreakers rather than betray our faith? At what price are we willing to take the cross into the world and identify with our Savior? How do we both love the people of the world and yet oppose the agenda of those who would crush the gospel?

When we come to the foot of the cross, it is there that we are finally broken; it is there that we learn to reach out to our confused and hurting world. The cross breaks down the barrier between us and the whole human race. Then we will no longer see ourselves as fighting the ACLU, the media, or the politicians. We must rid ourselves of the mentality that says, in effect, "If we just cleared all of them out, all would be well."[92]

I would like to leave you with GREAT HOPE. If you have become a believer in Jesus Christ, then you can watch for the return of Jesus with joyful expectation; be confident that the troubles of this world will take care of themselves.

"[34]Therefore do not worry about tomorrow, for tomorrow will worry about its own things. Sufficient for the day is its own trouble." (Matthew 6:34)

"[10]... wait for His Son [to return] from heaven, whom He raised from the dead, even Jesus who delivers us from the wrath to come." (1Thessalonians 1:10)

"[13]...looking for the blessed hope and glorious appearing of our great God and Savior Jesus Christ (Titus 2:13)

Here are a couple more quotations from Carolyn Leaf, that may help you cope with today's troubles:

"The way we react to things that happen to us is something we can change."

"A negative mind will never give you a positive life."

I am a proud American citizen, but my ultimate citizenship is in heaven. I am a child of the King waiting for His soon coming. You are too if you are a believer in Jesus.

"[20]For our citizenship is in heaven, from which we also eagerly wait for the Savior, the Lord Jesus Christ." (Philippians 3:20)

"[12]But as many as received Him, to them He gave the right to become children of God, to those who believe in His name." (John 1:12)

May God continue to Bless America and bless you!

Remember – the Rapture countdown continues. Jesus Christ is coming soon to collect his faithful flock.

Tic-Toc. Tic-Toc. Tic-Toc.

******

If you have enjoyed this book, please consider being kind enough to give it a good review. Please go to Amazon and pull up the book. Then scroll down and on the left side until the box "Write a customer review" appears. If you have not written a review before, simply state you enjoyed the book and recommend it. It is that simple.

The next book in this series is *The U.S.A. IN END TIME BIBLE PROPHECY: Blood Moons, Solar Eclipses, and The Revelation 12 Sign, Volume 3.* Jesus said, "And there will be signs in the sun, in the moon, and in the stars..." Today, millions of people believe the incredible number of celestial signs we are experiencing are a warning from God. What do these signs mean for America? What happens if we don't recognize these phenomena as signs from God? This is a timely book everyone needs to read!

The first book in this series is *The U.S.A. In End Time Bible Prophecy: Elections, Critical Race Theory, and Wokeness Alter Our Future*, Volume 1. America's role is limited in End Times events. How can this happen? Clues exist in the Bible that reveal the changes that will alter America's future.

If you have not read any of the following books in the End of the World series, please consider reading them. They have a lot of good information in them that is not normally taught in churches today.

How and When the World Ends, Volume 1. Analyzing Jewish idioms and Jesus' words reveal the day of the Rapture and when the Tribulation and End Times start.

End Time Rapture Signs: How and When the World Ends, Volume 2. Learn to recognize End Time signs, and have hope during these stressful times.

The Date of the Rapture: How and When the World Ends, Volume 3. A probable date of the Rapture and alternative dates are presented.

Revelation and Daniel Reveal How and When the World Ends, Volume 4. Prophetic scriptures pertaining to the Tribulation, the twenty-one plagues in Revelation, the Millennium judgment, and God's final promises to be fulfilled in the Millennium are discussed.

Heaven, Millennium, and Eternity, Volume 5. Gain insight into the changing environments and roles the saints experience as they transition from one eternal place to the next. The overriding theme of this book is HOPE for believers to live in peace from now to Eternity.

The Realignment of Nations for Armageddon: A New World Order Arises Hamas, Iran, Russia, China - Israel, Volume 6. This is the final book in this series and was released in November 2023. The Bible depicts multiple wars that potentially precede the last battle at Armageddon. The Russia – Ukraine war has caused a disruption of national alliances. Hamas attacked Israel on October 7, 2023. A new world order is being formed. Will this new world order form an alliance against Israel? This book discusses multiple interpretations of prominent author's views on these wars. It is designed to be like a road map for future events.

Concluding Thoughts

God allows humanity to exercise their free will to accept or reject Jesus as our Lord and Savior, but each of us is responsible for our own choice.

Have you made the commitment to accept Jesus as your Savior by turning away from your sins and asking Jesus to come into your life?

If you have not, here is a short explanation of The Four Spiritual Laws that will guide you in your decision to accept Jesus as your Savior.

1. God loves you and offers a wonderful plan for your life.

> *"[16]For God so loved the world that he gave his one and only Son, that whoever believes in him shall not perish but have eternal life." (John 3:16)*

> *"[10]The thief comes only to steal and kill and destroy; I have come that they may have life, and have it abundantly." (John 10:10)*

2. Man is sinful and separated from God. Therefore, man cannot know and experience God's love and plan for his life.

> *"[23]...for all have sinned and fall short of the glory of God." (Romans 3:23)*

> *"[23]For the wages of sin is death, but the gift of God is eternal life in Christ Jesus our Lord." (Romans 6:23)*

3. Jesus Christ is God's only provision for man's sin. Through him you can know and experience God's love and plan for your life.

> *"[8]But God demonstrates his own love for us in this: While we were still sinners, Christ died for us." (Romans 5:8)*

> *"[6]I am the way and the truth and the life. No one comes to the Father except through me." (John 14:6)*

4. We must individually receive Jesus Christ as Savior and Lord; then we can know and experience God's love and plan for our lives

> "[12]Yet to all who did receive him, to those who believed in his name, he gave the right to become children of God." (John 1:12)

> "[3]Jesus replied, "Very truly I tell you, no one can see the kingdom of God unless they are born again."

> [4]How can someone be born when they are old?" Nicodemus asked. "Surely they cannot enter a second time into their mother's womb to be born!"

> [5]Jesus answered, Very truly I tell you, no one can enter the kingdom of God unless they are born of water and the Spirit. [6]Flesh gives birth to flesh, but the Spirit gives birth to spirit." (John 3:3-6)

> "[8]For it is by grace you have been saved, through faith—and this is not from yourselves, it is the gift of God - [9]not by works, so that no one can boast." (Ephesians 2:8-9)

> "[20]Here I am! I stand at the door and knock. If anyone hears my voice and opens the door, I will come in and eat with that person, and they with me." (Revelation 3:20).

If you are ready to ask Jesus to come into your heart, simply pray to God and ask that your sins be forgiven. Then ask Jesus to come into your heart and save you. That is all it takes!

If you prayed this prayer, you will now be able to spend Eternity with Father God and Jesus. Your life will be filled with hope!

I encourage you to find a local church you can call your "home" church to strengthen you in your walk with God, Jesus, and the Holy Spirit.

Then live for Him. Study His ways and follow His commands to "love God and love people."

A Thank You From the Author

Dear reader,

It is with sincere gratitude that I would like to thank you for reading *The U.S.A. in End Times Bible Prophecy: The Roles of Big Tech, Big Media, and Big Government.* We are living in trying and difficult times. I hope this book has provided you with peace and comfort and an expectation of the wonderful eternity all believers will experience.

If you have enjoyed this book, please consider being kind enough to give it a good review. Please go to Amazon and pull up the book. Then scroll down and on the left side until the box "Write a customer review" appears. If you have not written a review before, simply state you enjoyed the book and recommend it. It is that simple.

Please consider reading my other books listed before the Bibliography.

Please feel free to contact me at: *erbrist@gmail.com*

May God greatly bless you and keep you safe!

Earl Bristow

Glossary of Terms

Antichrist can be a person or force who opposes God's kingdom. The Antichrist is represented in Daniel and Revelation as the beast ten horns representing ten kings who comprise an evil empire battling against God. In the middle of the Tribulation, the Antichrist will destroy the harlot religion. When the Antichrist declares he is God, then Satan probably takes control of his mind and body.

Apocalypse in biblical terms speaks of the return of Jesus to rescue His people. For non-believers and society in general, the apocalypse has come to mean the complete and final destruction of the world.

Battle of Armageddon is a war like the world has never experienced before. On this dark day, Jesus comes the second time as the warrior King of Kings and the Lord of Lords. He destroys the enemies of Israel, establishes His kingdom, and begins His 1,000-year reign on this Earth

Beast of Sea or Another Beast comes out of the sea and is symbolic of the false prophet who is only called another beast once. Every other time he is called the false prophet.

Believer in Christ (or Jesus), *saved* and *born* again have interchangeable meanings in this book. The definitions vary by denomination, so I am going to keep this simple and apply the following descriptions to each of these words. Any person who acknowledges and believes in their heart:

- God is the Father, Jesus Christ is the Son of God, and the Holy Spirit are one triune being.

- Jesus is the sacrificial Lamb of God who chose to die on the cross to atone for our sins so we could be in right standing with God the Father.

- After Jesus died, He rose from the dead, descended into Hades, then ascended into Heaven where He resides at the right hand of God the Father.

- Jesus will return to Earth to unite with all believers who have died and those who are alive. He will judge the non-believers.

Bride (of Christ) is a believer in Christ and is also a part of the Church.

Bridegroom is a term used to represent Jesus.

Church refers to all people worldwide who believe Jesus is the Son of God.

Day of the Lord describes the series of events by which Jesus gives the final call to believe in Him, brings judgment upon sin, and brings about a perfect eternal state. This includes the Tribulation, His Second Coming, the Millennial Kingdom, the Great White Throne Judgment, and the establishment of the New Heaven and New Earth.

Dragon is always symbolic of Satan.

End Times refers to the period in modern times when the end times events prophesied by Jesus begin to unfold with signs increasing in frequency e.g., wars, rumors of war, famines, diseases (pestilences), and earthquakes. The key to the start of the End Times was the rebirth of the nation of Israel in 1948.

Eternity is the last dimension of God's plan for humanity. It begins after the Millennial reign of Jesus, and it has no end.

First beast is symbolic of the Antichrist and comes out of the earth in Revelation. In Daniel the first beast was also symbolic of King Nebuchadnezzar.

First Coming is the thirty-three years of Jesus' birth, life, death, and resurrection on Earth approximately 2,000 years ago. Jesus ascended into Heaven to complete His First Coming.

Gentile is any person who is not Jewish.

Great Harlot or Harlot of Babylon is the term used throughout the Bible as a metaphor for false religion. The harlot is neither the Antichrist nor the false prophet. The harlot refers to another person, possibly persons, in charge of this religious institution.

Great White Throne Judgment is God's final judgment upon humanity, coming after the Millennium. Every person whose name is not found in Christ's Book of Life (i.e., nonbelievers) is already condemned, doomed to an eternity in the lake of fire. This sentencing hearing considers the good and evil deeds recorded in the books of heaven. The severity of punishment for each nonbeliever is determined at this judgment.

Heaven is a place for believers to live a life in redeemed bodies and experience love and peace beyond all understanding. The beauty, glory, and splendor are beyond description. Saints will continually worship and praise God while thanking Him for all He has done.

Hell is eternal separation from God in an eternal lake of fire. Non-believers in Jesus will be eternally separated from God because of their non-belief and unconfessed sins.

Little horn is the *little horn* that rises from the head of the terrifying beast in Daniel 7:8. The little horn represents the Antichrist in future time when the Antichrist establishes and controls a one-world religious system through the false prophet.

Millennium is the thousand-year reign of Jesus here upon this earth. It starts after the Tribulation and ends after 7,000 years. It is followed by Eternity. It is also referred to as the Millennial Kingdom.

New Heaven and New Earth will be the eternal dwelling places of believers in Jesus Christ. The new heaven and new earth are sometimes referred to as the "eternal state" for believers.

Rapture is the event when Jesus will appear in the sky above the Earth and summon up to Him in Heaven all the dead who believed in Him and all the true believers actively in a relationship with Jesus who are alive on Earth. His appearance at this time is *not* His Second Coming.

The word Rapture evolved from the Latin word *rapiemur*. The word harpazo in the Greek has the same meaning. The word *harpazo* means to seize, to snatch, to catch up or to carry away. The use of the word Rapture has become a popular and correct replacement for the phrase *"caught up."*

The purpose of the Rapture is to save the church, or body of Christ, from the wrath of God that comes during the seven years of Tribulation. Jesus will not be visible to the non-believers when He returns. The impact of millions of people instantly vanishing into the air will have a profound impact on those left behind. The Rapture triggers the start of the Tribulation.

Saints are New Testament believers – they can be alive or in heaven

Satan was created as one of the cherubims and held a position of great authority. God possibly placed him in charge of all creation since he was in the Garden of Eden. Satan was cast out of heaven because of his sin (Ezekiel 28:11-16). Satan's downfall came from his pride by declaring he would ascend into heaven and exalt his throne above the stars of God (Isaiah 14:13).

Through deceit and trickery, he caused Eve to eat of the forbidden fruit. This brought sin into the world of humanity.

Currently, Satan is *"the prince of the power of the air"* (Ephesians 2:2) and has a vast host of demons (Matthew 7:22) committed to him. Satan has the power of death upon earth (Hebrews 2:14). He still has access to God as the *"accuser of our brothers"* (Revelation 12:10) and continues to bring sin and wickedness into the world.

At the beginning of the Great Tribulation Satan's access to God as accuser will be withdrawn and Satan is removed from Heaven. Satan turns his attention to the earth and wreaks havoc during the last half of the Tribulation and especially on the Jews. At the Battle of Armageddon, Satan and his demons are defeated and cast into the Lake of Fire for 1,000 years. At the end of the 1,000 years, he is released for a short while, and is defeated again. He is then cast forever into the Lake of Fire

Second Coming of Jesus refers to the instance where Jesus physically returns to Earth after the seven years of Tribulation have been completed. He physically steps onto the Mount of Olives and is seen by all.

Seven heads are seven empires from history that persecuted Israel: Egypt, Assyria, Babylon, Persia, Greece, Rome, and the revived Roman Empire.

Sheol is the Old Testament word for the abode of the dead. It refers to the state or abode of the dead.

Ten horns represent a future ten nation confederation of ten kings that rule simultaneously together under the Antichrist's authority. The common belief is these nations will come of the European Union (EU), or they will take over the E.U.

Tanakh is an acronym of the first Hebrew letter of each of the three traditional subdivisions of the Torah (*'Teaching,'* also known as the *Five Books of Moses*), Nevi'im (*'Prophets'*) and Ketuvim (*'Writings'*) therefore, the name TaNaKh.

Torah, Talmud, Mishnah – The ***Torah*** is the Hebrew Bible, and while some people think of just the Five Books of Moses as being the Torah. *Torah* refers to all the Hebrew Bible, including such books as Joshua, Psalms, Book of Ruth, etc. The ***Talmud*** is the compilation of the historic rabbis *"discussing"* or *"debating"* what the *Torah* means.

Talmud is Hebrew for *"learning,"* appropriate for a text that people devote their lives to studying and mastering.

> ***Mishnah*** is the main text of the Talmud, a collection of teachings written in Hebrew, redacted by Rabbi Yehuda the Prince, in the years following the destruction of the Second Temple in Jerusalem in 70 A.D.

Tribulation is a future seven-year period beginning either immediately or a short time after the Rapture. Since the Rapture has taken all the true believers from the Earth, the remaining people on Earth do not believe in Jesus. At this time, God initiates a series of plagues bringing death and destruction in hopes the non-believers will repent and turn to Him. The Tribulation is often referred to as the *"Time of Jacob's Troubles"* because of the unparalleled amount of suffering the Jewish people endure for the rejection of their Messiah, Jesus.

Wedding, Divorce, and Marriage

God instructed the writers of the Bible to use terminology, imagery, metaphors, and similes to aid understanding of His instructions. One of the most prominent Bible metaphors in both the Old and New Testaments is the Jewish wedding process. The Old Testament comparison is a man and a woman entering an engagement and marriage. This marriage is like the relationship between the nation of Israel and God. Because of its unfaithfulness, God rejects and divorces Israel. Jeremiah describes the divorce:

> *"Then I saw that for all the causes for which backsliding Israel had committed adultery,* **I had put her away and given her a certificate of divorce**; *yet her treacherous sister Judah did not fear, but went and played the harlot also." (Jeremiah 3:8)*

The New Testament metaphor describes in detail the pending wedding of the bridegroom, Jesus, to His bride, the Church. God terminated (divorced) the relationship with Israel when Jesus became the sacrifice for our sins, which ended the Old Testament Jewish laws. Every person, including all Jews who fail to enter the marriage contract with Jesus, faces eternal consequences.

Books By Earl Bristow

How and When the World Ends, Volume 1. Jewish idioms are analyzed and Jesus' words reveal the day of the Rapture and when the Tribulation and end times start.

End Time Rapture Signs: How and When the World Ends, Volume 2. Learn to recognize End Time signs, and have hope during these stressful times.

The Date of the Rapture: How and When the World Ends, Volume 3. A probable date of the Rapture and alternative dates are presented.

Revelation and Daniel Reveal How and When the World Ends, Volume 4. Prophetic scriptures pertaining to the Tribulation, the twenty-one plagues in Revelation, the Millennium judgment, and God's final promises to be fulfilled in the Millennium are discussed.

Heaven, Millennium, and Eternity, Volume 5. Gain insight into the changing environments and roles the saints experience as they transition from one eternal place to the next. The overriding theme of this book is HOPE for believers to live in peace from now to Eternity.

The Realignment of Nations for Armageddon: A New World Order Arises Hamas, Iran, Russia, China - Israel, Volume 6. This is the final book in this series and was released in November 2023. The Bible depicts multiple wars that potentially precede the last battle at Armageddon. The Russia – Ukraine war has caused a disruption of national alliances. Hamas attacked Israel on October 7, 2023. A new world order is being formed. Will this new world order form an alliance against

Israel? This book discusses multiple interpretations of prominent author's views on these wars. It is designed to be like a road map for future events.

The U.S.A. In End Time Bible Prophecy: Elections, Critical Race Theory, and Wokeness Alter Our Future, Volume 1. America's role is limited in End Times events. How can this happen? Clues exist in the Bible that reveal the changes that will alter America's future.

The U.S.A. In End Times Bible Prophecy: The Roles of Big Tech, Big Media, and Big Government, Volume 2. This book describes the impact Big Tech, Big Media, and Big Government have on the U.S. in End Times. God has a plan that permits Satan to play a major role in the U.S. I think you will find it interesting reading.

The U.S.A. IN END TIME BIBLE PROPHECY: Blood Moons, Solar Eclipses, and The Revelation 12 Sign, Volume 3. Jesus said, "And there will be signs in the sun, in the moon, and in the stars…" Today, millions of people believe the incredible number of celestial signs we are experiencing are a warning from God. What do these signs mean for America? What happens if we don't recognize these phenomena as signs from God? This is a timely book everyone needs to read!

EARL BRISTOW BOOKS

Endnotes / Bibliography

It is important to note I do not endorse all the content in these books or websites. It is equally important to note they **DO NOT** endorse the work in my book either. Below are books and web sites relevant to this book.

---

[1] https://www.sciencedaily.com/releases/2000/06/000628101549.htm

[2] https://en.wikipedia.org/wiki/The_Perfect_Storm_(film)

[3] https://en.wikipedia.org/wiki/Hurricane_Grace

[4] https://en.wikipedia.org/wiki/The_Perfect_Storm_(film)

[5] https://www.usnews.com/news/health-news/articles/2023-03-01/fbi-director-says-covid-19-origin-is-most-likely-a-lab-incident-in-china

[6] https://www.newsweek.com/2021/08/13/doomsday-covid-variant-worse-delta-lambda-may-coming-scientists-say-1615874.html

[7] https://www.statista.com/statistics/1299985/voice-assistant-users-us/

[8] https://www.history.com/this-day-in-history/the-boston-tea-party

[9] https://history.house.gov/People/Continental-Congress/Continental-Confederation-Congresses/

[10] https://www.history.com/news/how-the-great-compromise-affects-politics-today

[11] https://en.wikipedia.org/wiki/United_States_Bill_of_Rights

[12] https://en.wikipedia.org/wiki/Pre-Marxist_communism

[13] https://www.pewresearch.org/short-reads/2023/07/19/what-the-data-says-

about-food-stamps-in-the-u-s/

[14]https://americanpromise.net/2019/04/5-reasons-we-need-an-amendment-to-say-corporations-arent-people/?gclid=CjwKCAjwj8eJBhA5EiwAg3z0m3yPhS9ahgY1AzzvR9VXfaRq_ydmIc-P64u6X-0x8bGoTFdPFwC__RoCU4EQAvD_BwE

[15]https://www.washingtonpost.com/politics/2021/06/22/technology-202-biden-administration-full-officials-who-worked-prominent-tech-companies/

[16]https://www.eternalgod.org/would-you-please-explain-daniel-124-stating-that-many-shall-run-to-and-fro-and-knowledge-shall-increase/

[17]https://en.wikipedia.org/wiki/History_of_transport

[18]https://www.ncsl.org/research/transportation/autonomous-vehicles-self-driving-vehicles-enacted-legislation.aspx#:~:text=Twenty%2Dnine%20states%E2%80%94Alabama%2C,%2C%20Virginia%2C%20Vermont%2C%20Washington%20and

[19]https://en.wikipedia.org/wiki/Internet_of_things

[20]https://www.pewresearch.org/science/2023/05/16/what-americans-think-about-covid-19-vaccines/

[21]https://www.haaretz.com/us-news/republican-lawmaker-says-biden-s-covid-vaccine-staff-are-needle-nazis-1.9987915

[22]https://www.businessnewsdaily.com/in-office-covid-vaccine-requirements

[23]https://www.pewresearch.org/short-reads/2023/07/19/what-the-data-says-about-food-stamps-in-the-u-s/

[24]https://www.atlanticcouncil.org/cbdctracker/

[25]https://www.federalreserve.gov/faqs/is-fednow-replacing-cash-is-it-a-central-bank-digital-currency.htm

[26]https://tectales.com/bio-tech-it/tiny-injectable-chips-use-ultrasound-for-monitoring.html

[27]https://www.livescience.com/20718-computer-history.html

[28]https://www.ibm.com/topics/quantum-computing

[29]https://www.softwaretestinghelp.com/artificial-intelligence-software/

[30]https://www.zdnet.com/article/could-quantum-networking-rescue-the-communications-industry-status-report/

[31]https://platinumdatarecovery.com/blog/6-emerging-trends-of-data-storage-technology

[32]https://en.wikipedia.org/wiki/Technological_singularity

[33]ttps://techcrunch.com/2023/03/28/1100-notable-signatories-just-signed-an-open-letter-asking-all-ai-labs-to-immediately-pause-for-at-least-6-months/

[34]https://www.linkedin.com/pulse/you-getting-obsolete-arif-hassan

[35]https://time.com/5955412/artificial-intelligence-nvidia-jensen-huang/

[36]https://www.jpost.com/arab-israeli-conflict/gaza-news/guardian-of-the-walls-the-first-ai-war-669371

[37]https://iapp.org/news/a/china-leading-on-ai-regulation/

[38]https://www.washingtonpost.com/technology/2021/07/07/ai-weapons-us-military/

[39]https://www.tidio.com/blog/chat-gpt/

[40]https://www.statista.com/topics/3196/social-media-usage-in-the-united-states/#topicOverview

[41]https://datareportal.com/reports/digital-2023-china

[42]https://datareportal.com/reports/digital-2023-russian-federation

[43]https://www.worldometers.info/world-population/europe-population/

[44]https://www.statista.com/forecasts/715683/e-commerce-users-in-europe

[45] https://www.fastcompany.com/90636859/the-volume-of-the-problem-is-astonishing-amazons-battle-against-fakes-may-be-too-little-too-late

[46] https://news.microsoft.com/bythenumbers/en/windowsdevices

[47] https://blog.mailfence.com/big-tech/

[48] https://www.cdc.gov/vaccines/covid-19/reporting/requirements/index.html

[49] https://www.who.int/publications/i/item/WHO-2019-nCoV-Digital_certificates-vaccination-2021.1

[50] https://pressgazette.co.uk/media-audience-and-business-data/media_metrics/top-25-us-newspaper-circulations-down-march-2023/

[51] https://en.wikipedia.org/wiki/News_broadcasting#:~:text=Today%20was%20the%20first%20morning,Network%20from%201947%20to%201948.

[52] https://www.pewresearch.org/fact-tank/2021/01/12/more-than-eight-in-ten-americans-get-news-from-digital-devices/

[53] https://prpioneer.com/post/who-owns-the-news-a-close-look-at-online-sources-in-america

[54] https://en.wikipedia.org/wiki/Twitter_under_Elon_Musk

[55] https://en.wikipedia.org/wiki/Restrictions_on_TikTok_in_the_United_States

[56] https://www.pareteum.com/37-statistics-to-know-about-the-sms-market-in-2021/

[57] https://www.askdavetaylor.com/what_is_define_fourth_estate_fifth_column/

[58] https://en.wikipedia.org/wiki/Disinformation_Governance_Board

[59] https://theintercept.com/2022/10/31/social-media-disinformation-dhs/

[60] https://thehill.com/opinion/technology/4091216-bidens-social-media-manipulation-is-exactly-what-the-framers-feared/

[61] https://www.politifact.com/factchecks/2023/jan/10/scott-perry/fbi-doj-

tagged-threats-against-school-officials-no/

[62]https://www.catholicnewsagency.com/news/255053/house-judiciary-committee-multiple-fbi-field-offices-involved-with-anti-catholic-memo

[63]https://www.fdrlibrary.org/great-depression-facts

[64]https://www.history.com/topics/great-depression/new-deal

[65]https://www.americanactionforum.org/research/tracker-paycheck-protection-program-loans/#:~:text=Congress%20later%20provided%20an%20additional,the%20PPP%20to%20%24669%20billion.

[66]https://www.cnn.com/2023/08/11/economy/inflation-rate-spending/index.html

[67]https://www.brennancenter.org/our-work/research-reports/citizens-united-explained

[68]https://www.forbes.com/sites/michelatindera/2021/02/25/these-billionaire-donors-spent-the-most-money-on-the-2020-election/?sh=11c3fbbf14ce

[69]https://www.nytimes.com/2021/05/03/us/politics/hansjorg-wyss-money-democrats.html

[70]https://www.lawofficer.com/george-soros-donates-to-an-organization-to-defund-police-as-crime-spikes/

[71]https://www.washingtonpost.com/opinions/2023/03/13/biden-budget-socialism-lost/

[72]https://www.dataforprogress.org/blog/2022/1/26/democratic-socialism-and-socialism-are-increasingly-salient-among-democrats

[73]https://nclalegal.org/biden-executive-orders/

[74]https://www.npr.org/2021/08/26/1024668578/court-blocks-biden-cdc-evictions-moratorium

[75]https://www.cbsnews.com/news/eviction-ban-national-apartment-

association-sues-federal-government-for-back-rent/

[76]https://www.wsj.com/articles/covid-19s-toll-on-u-s-business-200-000-extra-closures-in-pandemics-first-year-11618580619

[77]https://www.statesman.com/story/news/politics/politifact/2021/06/08/kamala-harris-small-business-closures-covid-fact-check/7602531002/

[78]https://amc.sas.upenn.edu/francis-fukuyama-against-identity-politics

[79]https://en.wikipedia.org/wiki/Great_Reset

[80]https://www.wsj.com/articles/federal-agencies-use-cellphone-location-data-for-immigration-enforcement-11581078600

[81]https://irp.fas.org/budget/index.html

[82]https://www.thebalance.com/interest-on-the-national-debt-4119024

[83]https://finance.yahoo.com/news/20-cuts-social-security-may-123017196.html

[84]https://www.pewresearch.org/fact-tank/2021/08/16/americas-incarceration-rate-lowest-since-1995/

[85]https://en.wikipedia.org/wiki/List_of_wars_by_death_toll

[86]https://www.wsj.com/articles/the-world-relies-on-one-chip-maker-in-taiwan-leaving-everyone-vulnerable-11624075400

[87]https://www.actionagainsthunger.org/world-hunger-facts-statistics

[88]https://en.wikipedia.org/wiki/Spanish_flu

[89]https://www.insurancejournal.com/news/national/2021/06/15/618657.htm

[90]https://www.timesnownews.com/explainer/11-major-earthquakes-in-2022-is-a-big-one-coming-and-can-it-be-predicted-and-what-are-megaquakes-article-95760016

[91]https://www.statista.com/statistics/263104/worldwide-earthquakes-since-

2006-by-richter-scale-gradation/

[92]Lutzer, Erwin W., *When A Nation Forgets God*, Moody Publishers, Chicago, Illinois 2010, Kindle eBook locations 375-385

Made in the USA
Monee, IL
17 March 2024